A DAY
IN THE LIFE OF
YOUR BODY

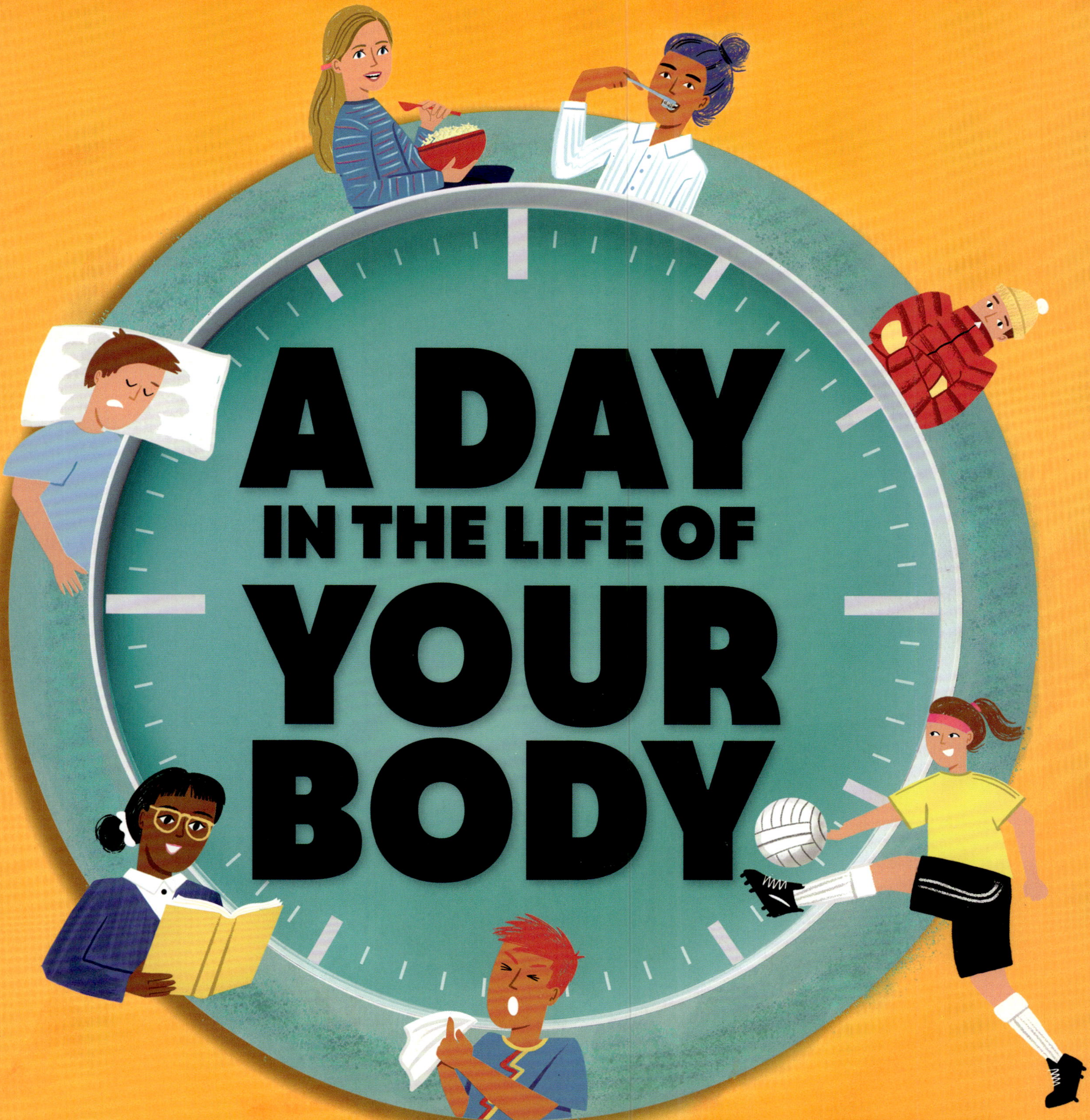

A DAY IN THE LIFE OF YOUR BODY

Illustrated by Liz Kay and Amy Grimes

Project Editor Vicky Richards
Senior Designer Sheila Collins
Editors Binta Jallow, Anna Streiffert Limerick
Designers Beth Johnston, Mik Gates
Managing Editor Francesca Baines
Managing Art Editor Philip Letsu
US Editor Kayla Dugger
Production Editor Dragana Puvacic
Production Controller Leanne Burke
Jacket Designer Sheila Collins
Jacket Illustrator Liz Kay
Publisher Andrew Macintyre
Art Director Mabel Chan

Illustrated by Liz Kay and Amy Grimes
Written by Binta Jallow, Vicky Richards, and Anna Streiffert Limerick

Consultant Dr. Kristina Routh

First published in Great Britain in 2025 by
Dorling Kindersley Limited
20 Vauxhall Bridge Road,
London SW1V 2SA

The authorised representative in the EEA is
Dorling Kindersley Verlag GmbH. Arnulfstr. 124,
80636 Munich, Germany

Copyright © 2025 Dorling Kindersley Limited
A Penguin Random House Company
10 9 8 7 6 5 4 3 2 1
001–341867–Oct/2025

All rights reserved.
No part of this publication may be reproduced, stored in or introduced into a retrieval system, or transmitted, in any form, or by any means (electronic, mechanical, photocopying, recording, or otherwise), without the prior written permission of the copyright owner.
No part of this publication may be used or reproduced in any manner for the purpose of training artificial intelligence technologies or systems. In accordance with Article 4(3) of the DSM Directive 2019/790, DK expressly reserves this work from the text and data mining exception.

A CIP catalogue record for this book
is available from the British Library.
ISBN: 978-0-2416-8319-4

Medway Libraries and Archives	
95600000334595	
Askews & Holts	
	£22.00
	ROC

CONTENTS

Rise and shine

Wake up	10
Feeling tired and grumpy	12
Morning scrub	14
Building blocks	16
Toothy grin	18
Tooth trouble	20
Breathe easy	22
The body up high	24
Hop, skip, and jump	26
Breakfast club	28
Snow day	30

On the move

On the run	34
Thirsty work	36
Queasy ride	38
The body in space	40
Art attack	42
Feeling anxious	44
Toilet time	46
Leap and twist	48
At the doctor's	50
First aid kit	52

Working hard

Watch, listen, and learn	56
Take a seat	58
Tricky tackle	60
Accidents happen	62
Grab a bite	64
Making music	66
Feeling envious	68
Chemical code	70
Make a splash	72
The body underwater	74

Winding down

Cooking up a storm	100
Feeling happy	102
Eat up	104
Time to digest	106
Microbes	108
Game on!	110
The body at high speed	112
Sleepover	114
On your skin	116
Sleep tight	118
Growing up	120

Time for a break

Got to go	78
At the museum	80
Catching up	82
Flower power	84
Allergies	86
Scary movie	88
Feeling sad	90
Celebrate!	92
Heatwave	94
Flying high	96

Body systems

Skeletal system and muscular system	124
Circulatory system and nervous system	126
Respiratory system and digestive system	128
Reproductive system and lymphatic system	130
Looking inside your body	132
Your day in numbers	134
Glossary	136
Index	140
Acknowledgements	144

HOW TO USE THIS BOOK

Travel through a single day
This book is made up of snapshots in the day of different children – from everyday eating and sleeping to exciting trips and events. Around each scene you'll find pictures and stories that reveal what is going on inside your body.

Tell the time with clocks that show you where you are in the day.

GRAB A BITE

Your mouth may water and your stomach rumble before you eat lunch. Be sure to chew each morsel well so it can travel down your throat to your stomach.

Look out for handy circles that show you where smaller parts of the body can be found.

Detailed diagrams explain how different body parts work.

Numbered steps help you to follow body processes.

Each unique event in the day has a cast of new children.

Small intestine

1. Intestine walls contract here.
2. This section relaxes.
3. Food moves along propelled by frequent waves of muscle contractions.

WHY CAN SPICY FOODS MAKE YOU FEEL LIKE YOUR MOUTH IS BURNING?
Spicy foods contain a substance called capsaicin. This triggers nerves in the mouth that normally detect heat, making your body think it is overheating. Your body attempts to clear out the cause of the problem by making you sweat, and get a runny nose, and your mouth may feel like it is burning!

WHY DOES YOUR STOMACH RUMBLE?
All parts of your digestive tract – from oesophagus to anus – have muscular walls that contract to constantly push food along. This process is known as peristalsis and may cause growling noises! It is thought that you especially hear noises when you are hungry, because the stomach and intestines have less food inside them to muffle the sounds.

64

Each story answers a key question about how your body works.

FIND OUT MORE

● **Zoom in**
Some pages have a special focus on the smallest parts of your body, such as tiny gut bacteria.

● **Extreme living**
Discover how your body would survive in space or underwater on special feature pages.

● **What's happening?**
Find out more about common body features, illnesses, and how to keep yourself healthy.

● **Pull it all together**
A reference section at the back of the book shows all of your body systems in one place, plus you'll find pages of fun facts!

WHY DOESN'T FOOD GO DOWN THE WRONG WAY?

To make sure your food does not end up in the lungs instead of the stomach, your throat changes shape when you swallow. A flap of cartilage called the epiglottis folds downwards, blocking the entrance to your windpipe. Part of the roof of your mouth also blocks air from the nose from entering until the food passes through.

Epiglottis folds down to prevent access to windpipe.
Food moves down the oesophagus.
Teeth
Windpipe

HOW DO YOU CHEW FOOD?

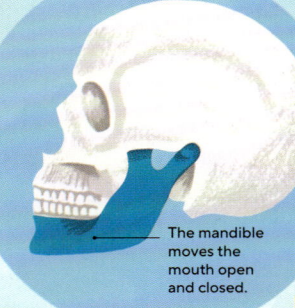

Most of the bones in your head are hard and immoveable, forming the skull, which protects the brain. But your lower jawbone, known as the mandible, is the only bone in the face that can move. Strong muscles (see page 104) pull it up and down, allowing your upper and lower teeth to meet with a powerful bite, crushing food between them.

The mandible moves the mouth open and closed.

Why can some people tolerate more spice than others?

Both nature and nurture are thought to affect how you feel about spicy food. Scientists think some people might have genes that help them tolerate higher levels of spice, but your spice sensitivity is also affected by how frequently you eat those kinds of food. Repeatedly eating spicy snacks will probably increase the level of heat you like.

Fact boxes answer related curious questions on the theme of the scene.

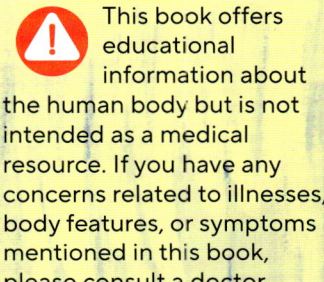

⚠ This book offers educational information about the human body but is not intended as a medical resource. If you have any concerns related to illnesses, body features, or symptoms mentioned in this book, please consult a doctor.

 # RISE AND SHINE

WAKE UP

You might barely remember your time sleeping, but your body has been busy during the night. As you stretch and yawn, it may take a bit of time to wake up and get going.

Hair strands

WHY IS YOUR HAIR MESSY IN THE MORNING?

You have lots of tiny individual hairs on your head. When you lie on the pillow, your hairs rub against it and each other, causing friction. This force can rough up the outermost part of the hair called the cuticle, which is made up of overlapping layers of dead cells. This produces the frizz you sometimes see!

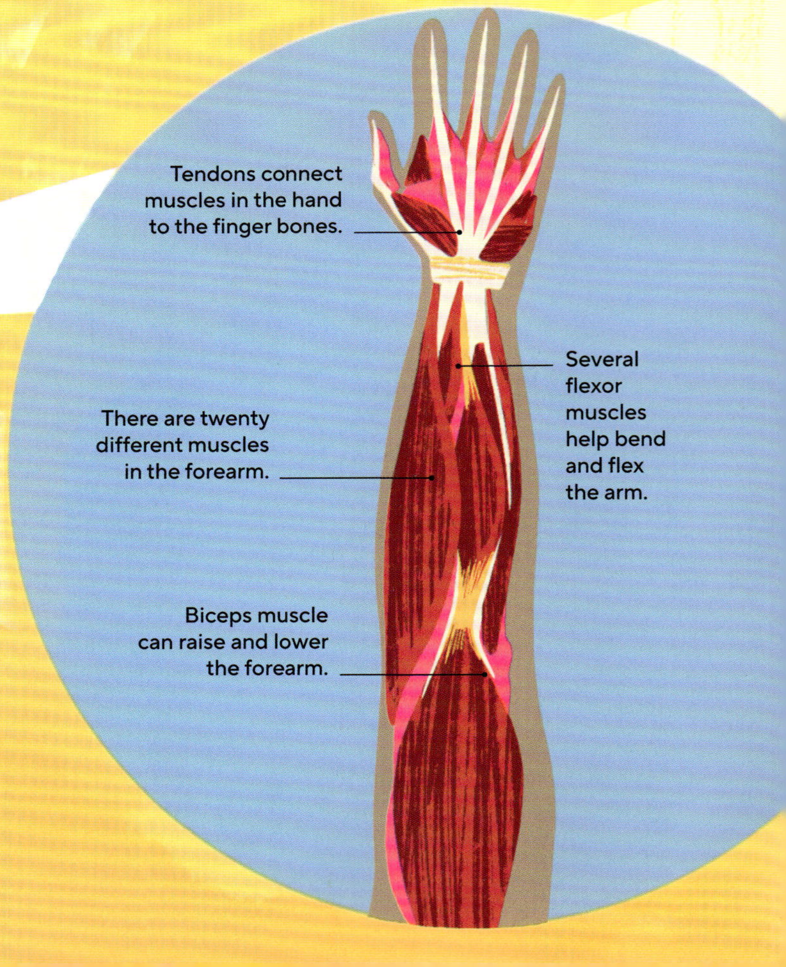

Overlapping layers of the cuticle form the outer protective part of the hair.

Tendons connect muscles in the hand to the finger bones.

There are twenty different muscles in the forearm.

Several flexor muscles help bend and flex the arm.

Biceps muscle can raise and lower the forearm.

10

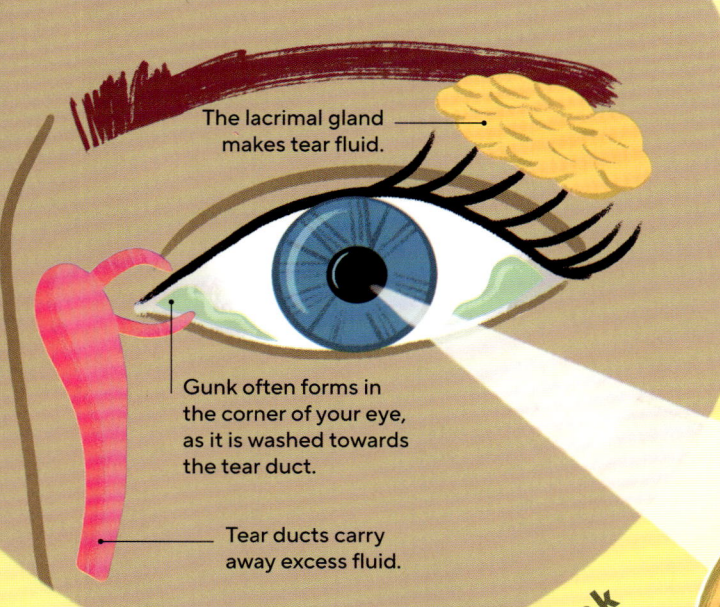

The lacrimal gland makes tear fluid.

Gunk often forms in the corner of your eye, as it is washed towards the tear duct.

Tear ducts carry away excess fluid.

Eye gunk

Mucus layer
Oily layer (meibum)
Watery layer

Tear layers

WHY DO YOU BLINK?

Each of your soft, squishy eyeballs needs to stay moist to see clearly. A gland under your eyebrow continually produces tear fluid to help with this. When you blink, this fluid is washed over the eye – preventing it from drying out and clearing away any irritating substances. New research also suggests blinking helps the brain process visual information.

WHY DO YOU GET GUNK IN YOUR EYE?

Your eyes are coated in a film made of three layers. The topmost layer is made of an oily substance called meibum. Normally, this prevents tears from spilling out and keeps our eyes moist. When you sleep, more meibum is produced and as the body cools, this hardens into the crusty gunk we wake up with.

1. Air enters through the mouth and nose as we yawn.
2. The muscles in the face, jaw, and neck stretch.
3. The throat enlarges.

WHAT MAKES YOU YAWN?

There are several theories about why we yawn. It could be to cool the body, allow more oxygen to enter the bloodstream, or to wake up the brain – making the body more alert. As you yawn, your jaw stretches open to its lowest position and air flows in.

Why are yawns so contagious?

Seeing someone else yawn can set you off, and scientists think this might be due to something called "social mirroring". This is where humans (and other animals) copy the behaviour of others in case it has a useful purpose.

WHY DO YOU STRETCH IN THE MORNING?

The stretching you do to wake your body up after sleep has a special name: pandiculation. As you reach your arms above your head, this sends oxygen and blood flowing towards your muscles – pulling on parts at the centre, called spindles. This stretches the muscles out and then allows them to spring back to their normal resting length, ready for the day ahead.

Why do you feel tired in the morning?

Being tired in the morning is normal and is often referred to as sleep inertia. This is when you feel groggy and disorientated not long after waking up. You might also think and react to things more slowly. Sleep inertia happens because our bodies are gradually transitioning from sleep to wakefulness.

Is it normal to feel grumpy in the morning?

It is quite common to feel a bit grouchy because you would like to sleep for longer. Children and teenagers need more sleep than adults, so being pulled from sleep earlier than you wanted can be especially difficult.

Why are some people better at mornings?

Some people prefer to go to bed early and wake up early while still feeling refreshed and well rested. The opposite of these "early birds" are "night owls" – people who are more energetic at night and tired in the morning. Which type of person you are depends on your genetics, as we are all born with our own natural sleep-wake cycle (circadian rhythm).

How can I feel less tired and grumpy?

- Try to ensure you get good quality sleep in a regular sleeping pattern by going to bed at the same time each day.

- Spend the first 30—60 minutes after waking outside or in a room with bright lights, to help your body wake up properly.

- If you're finding things stressful, look for ways to relax throughout the day, such as playing sports, doing calm activities such as reading or drawing, or doing breathing exercises.

How does sleep affect your mood?
Sleep plays an important role in keeping your emotions level, so when you sleep poorly, you're more likely to be irritable and stressed. You can also struggle to concentrate and may not have as much energy. Having a good night's sleep is associated with better wellbeing and good mental health.

What makes you feel angry?
Sometimes mild feelings of annoyance and frustration can grow into anger, when you feel cross with others or yourself. While feeling angry from time to time is normal, it can be helpful to look beneath the anger at what emotions have caused this reaction, such as sadness, fear, or shame.

FEELING TIRED AND GRUMPY

Spilled milk is just one side effect of morning grogginess. When a bad mood strikes, you may find yourself grumpy, irritable, or quick to get angry about the smallest things.

MORNING SCRUB

It's time to jump in the shower and freshen up for the day ahead. Before long, you'll be squeaky clean. But what's under your skin, and how do you keep it clean?

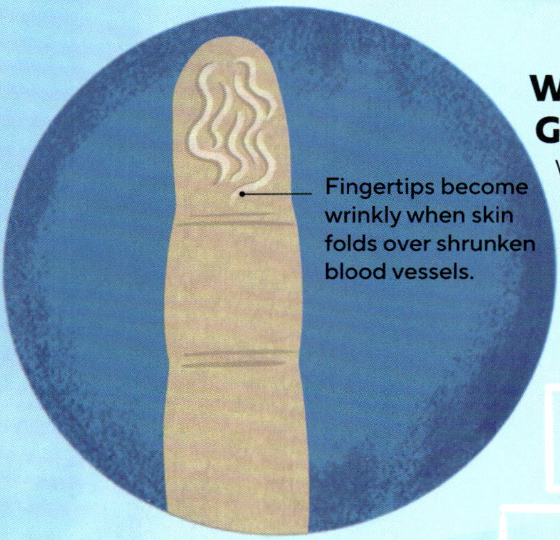

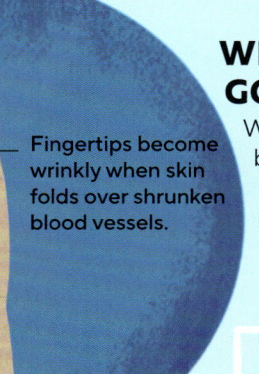

Fingertips become wrinkly when skin folds over shrunken blood vessels.

WHY DO YOUR FINGERS GO WRINKLY IN THE BATH?

When you're in water, your fingers turn wrinkly because your nervous system sends signals to the blood vessels in your fingertips, telling them to shrink. Scientists believe that our fingers wrinkle so we can pick up and grip underwater objects.

Why do your feet get smelly?

Your feet have more sweat glands than any other body part, so they can get very sweaty! But sweat only begins to smell when it is mixed with bacteria. Your sweaty feet are more likely to smell because they are often covered in socks and shoes, where lots of bacteria can quickly build up.

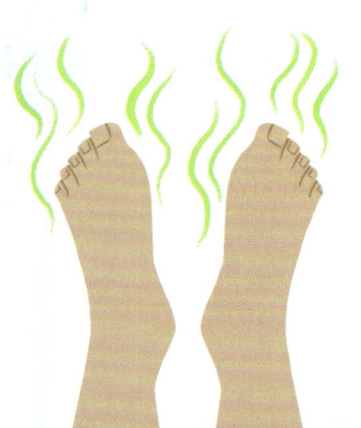

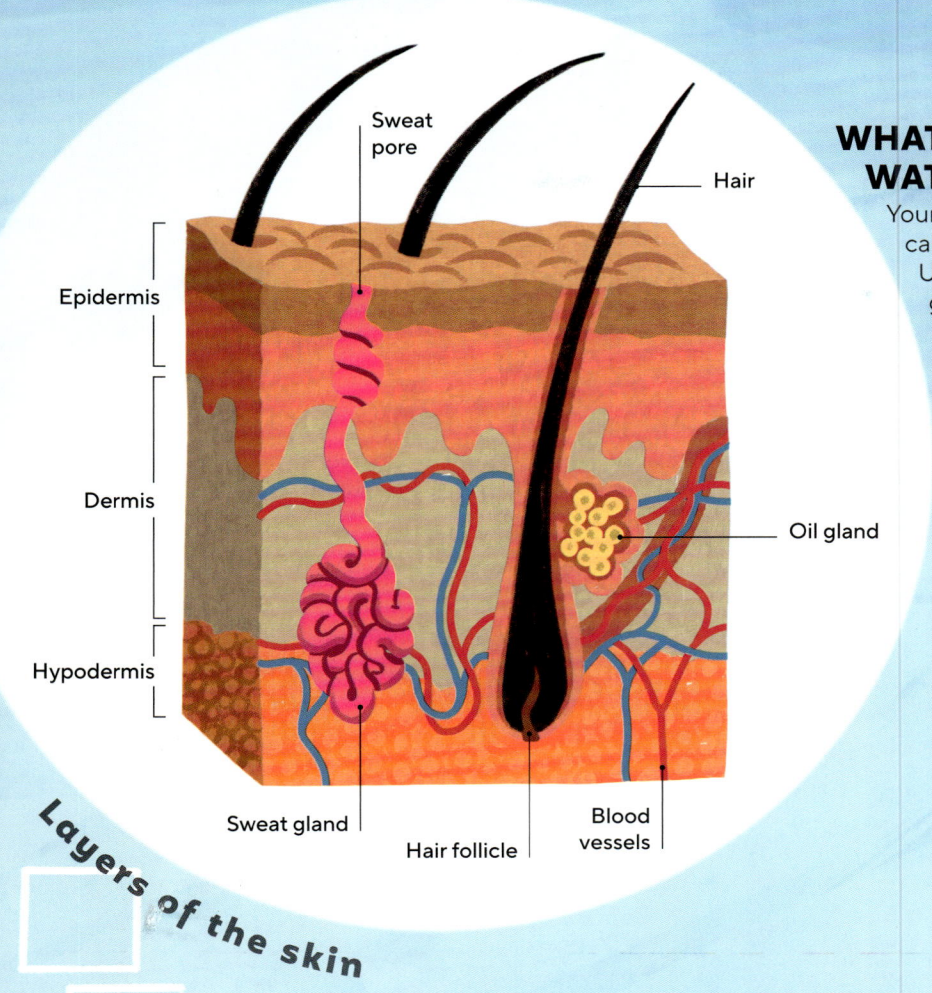

Layers of the skin

WHAT MAKES SKIN WATERPROOF?

Your skin has three main layers. The top layer, called the epidermis, is a protective barrier. Underneath is the dermis, which contains glands that produce oil. When this oil rises up alongside the hair shaft to the epidermis, our skin becomes waterproof because water cannot pass through an oily barrier. The bottom fatty layer of skin is called the hypodermis and helps keep us warm.

How does an antiperspirant work?

Antiperspirants reduce underarm sweat by creating a temporary plug over the sweat pores in your armpits. Unlike deodorants, which only get rid of the smell of body odour, antiperspirants stop both sweating and body odour.

How soap cleans

HOW DOES SOAP CLEAN YOUR SKIN?

When you mix soap with water, it creates a foamy lather that is easy to rub all over your body. The soap particles in this lather attach to dirt and oil, surrounding them and lifting them off the surface of your skin. When you rinse the foamy lather off, the dirt trapped inside the soap particles is washed away, too!

BUILDING BLOCKS

Your body is made of tiny units called cells. There are many different types of cells – from skin cells to nerve cells – all with their own shape, structure, and purpose.

ZOOMING OUT

Each cell is a tiny unit with its own function. But where in the body are cells found?

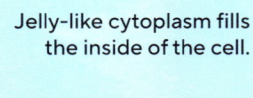

Jelly-like cytoplasm fills the inside of the cell.

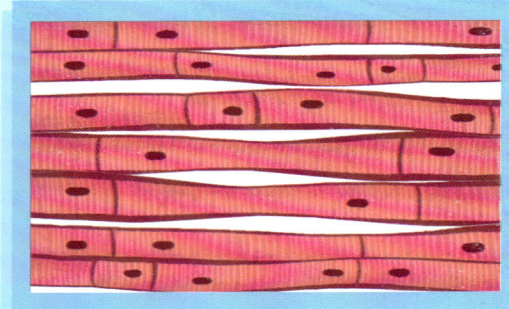

From tissue...
The walls of the heart are made of a type of tissue called cardiac muscle – constructed from rows of long individual muscle cells.

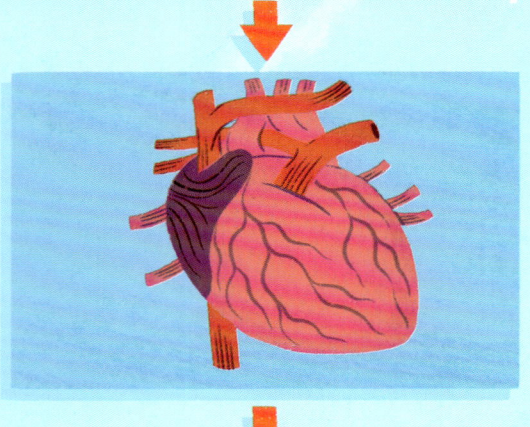

...to organs...
Your heart is the centre of your circulatory system. It is a powerful organ made of tissue that pumps blood around the body.

An outer membrane surrounds the cell and lets substances pass in and out.

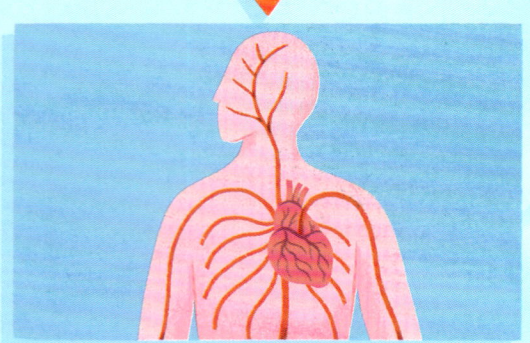

...to body systems
Your circulatory system (see page 126) extends throughout your whole body and is a network of busy blood vessels and your heart.

INSIDE A CELL
A microscopic cell is filled with even smaller structures called organelles, which work together as a living unit. These enable the cell to process the food it receives to release energy so that it can carry out its specific task in your body.

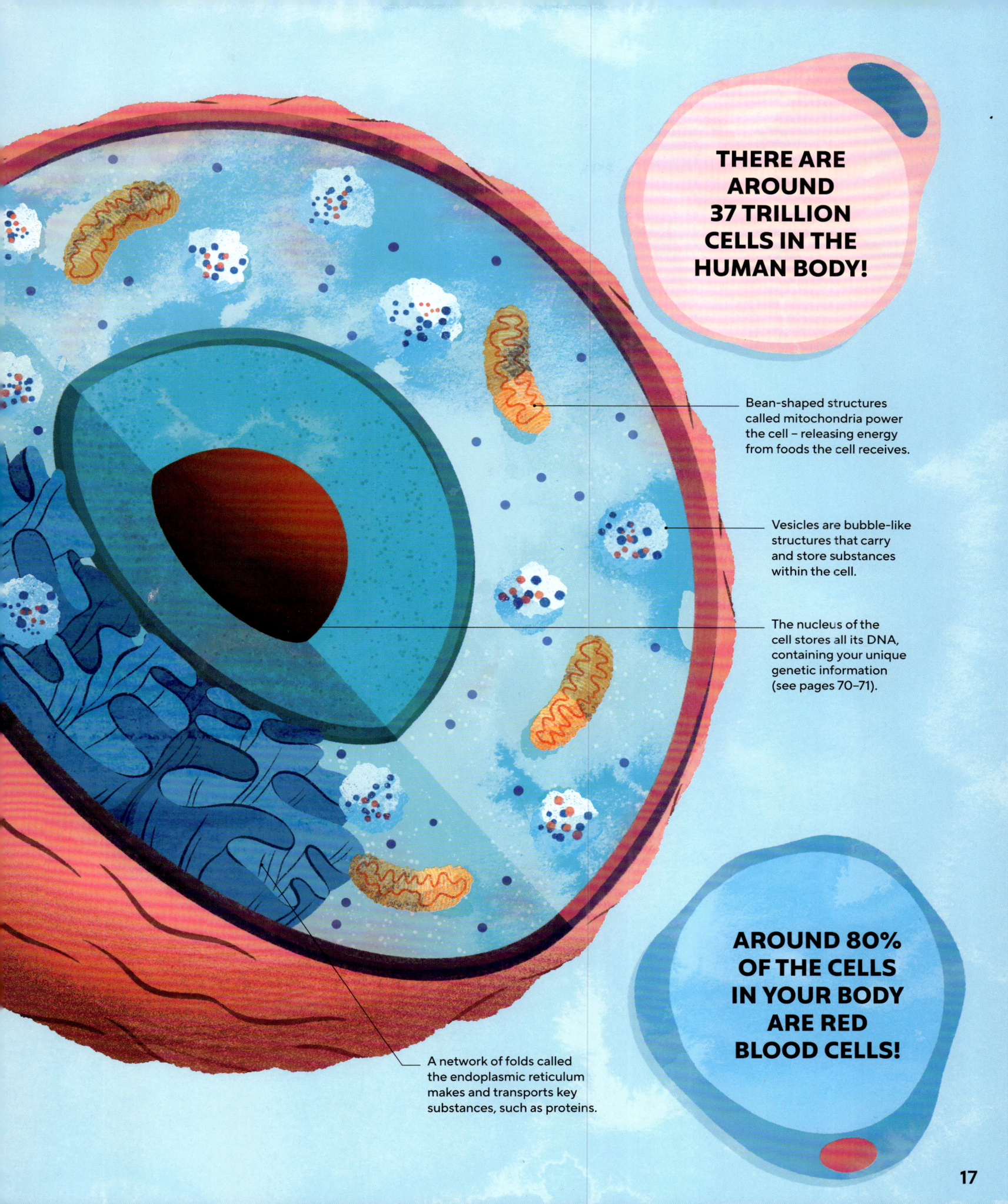

THERE ARE AROUND 37 TRILLION CELLS IN THE HUMAN BODY!

Bean-shaped structures called mitochondria power the cell – releasing energy from foods the cell receives.

Vesicles are bubble-like structures that carry and store substances within the cell.

The nucleus of the cell stores all its DNA, containing your unique genetic information (see pages 70–71).

A network of folds called the endoplasmic reticulum makes and transports key substances, such as proteins.

AROUND 80% OF THE CELLS IN YOUR BODY ARE RED BLOOD CELLS!

TOOTHY GRIN

The time to take care of your teeth, gums, and mouth comes around every morning (and night!), keeping your chewing tools in tip-top condition.

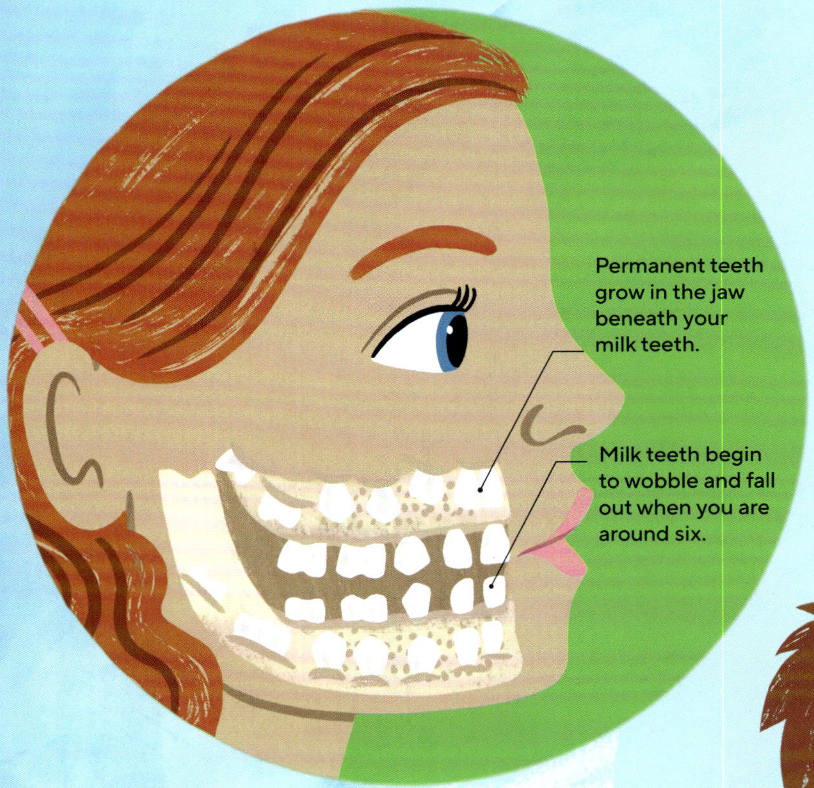

Permanent teeth grow in the jaw beneath your milk teeth.

Milk teeth begin to wobble and fall out when you are around six.

WHAT DOES BRUSHING YOUR TEETH DO?

Bacteria and food debris build up on your teeth as you eat and drink – hardening into a substance called plaque. Regularly brushing your teeth with a fluoride toothpaste is very important, as it helps to remove this plaque and prevent it from building up. Fluoride also protects against tooth decay.

Plaque may not be visible to the naked eye, but it builds up around the edges of teeth.

WHY DO SOME TEETH FALL OUT?

When you are young, your face and mouth are small, so your first set of teeth needs to be small too. As you get older, these teeth begin to wobble and fall out and are gradually replaced by the permanent teeth developing behind them in your jaw. These push through the gums to fill the space.

WHAT DO YOUR TONSILS DO?

These fleshy lumps at the back of your throat may not look important, but they are actually part of your immune system and play a role in fighting off harmful germs. Bacteria and viruses that enter through the mouth are filtered out of the air by the tissue of the tonsils. Tonsils can become enlarged due to infection and sometimes have to be removed.

Tonsils sit on either side of the back of your throat.

Soft tissue called the uvula blocks food from entering the nasal cavity.

Bumpy tongue surface

Bacteria and the gases they produce form a layer on top of the tongue.

Minuscule folds on the tongue's surface

WHAT CAUSES BAD BREATH?

It is normal to get bad breath sometimes. Often it is due to bacteria building up on the tongue, where they can get trapped on its bumpy, uneven surface. As these bacteria break down food, they release substances such as sulfur that give off a strong smell.

TOOTH TROUBLE

Your pearly whites aren't just for grinning, but are essential for a healthy mouth. It is important to regularly brush, floss, and get your teeth checked by a dentist to prevent problems.

BRACES
As your face and jaw grow, teeth can get overcrowded or overlap, and sometimes the teeth in your upper jaw and lower jaw do not align. Your dentist may suggest braces to help the teeth line up – most often metal brackets on the teeth or plastic retainers. These put pressure on your teeth to push them in the correct place, helping you both to eat and clean between the teeth more easily.

WISDOM TEETH
Although most of your teeth have emerged by your teen years, some teeth erupt through your gums a few years later. These teeth, which push up at the back of your mouth, are called wisdom teeth and can cause problems if they get trapped in the gums or come up at an angle. In these cases, a dentist might need to extract the tooth to prevent pain.

BRUSHING PROBLEMS

When plaque builds up on the teeth, it can sometimes irritate your gums, which may cause soreness and bleeding when you brush your teeth. Proper brushing and dental care can prevent this, but if you notice swelling in your gums, do see a dentist.

TOOTHACHE

A toothache is when your tooth or the area around it hurts. It can happen for lots of reasons, such as a wobbly tooth, a hole (cavity), or even an infection. Sometimes it goes away on its own, but if your toothache lasts more than two days or gets worse, it is important to see a dentist.

DENTAL CHECK UPS

It is important to visit the dentist to have regular check ups. During an appointment, a dentist will examine your teeth and gums to look for any potential problems. They may also clean between the teeth or take X-rays, which show them a clear view of all the teeth in your mouth.

BREATHE EASY

A quiet car journey can be a good place to prepare your body and mind for the day ahead. As you watch the world go by, take a deep breath and fill your lungs with air.

WHERE DOES THE AIR THAT YOU BREATHE IN GO?

Air that flows into your lungs travels through a network of branching tubes until it reaches tiny air sacs called alveoli. These have very thin walls and are where oxygen from the air passes into capillaries (blood vessels). At the same time, carbon dioxide passes back from the blood into the alveoli.

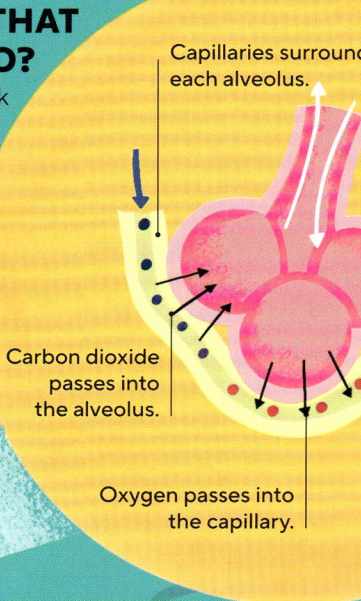

Gas exchange
- Capillaries surround each alveolus.
- Alveoli are tiny bags of air.
- Oxygen is carried away by the blood.
- Carbon dioxide passes into the alveolus.
- Oxygen passes into the capillary.

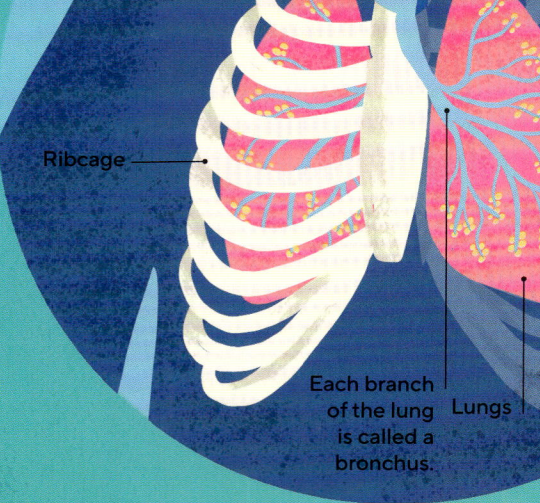

Ribcage
- Ribcage
- Each branch of the lung is called a bronchus.
- Lungs

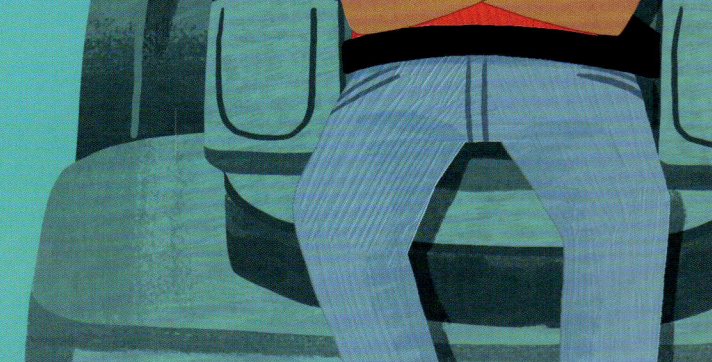

HOW OFTEN DO YOU NEED TO BREATHE?

A person's breathing rate depends on a range of things, from whether they are exercising to if they feel ill. But at normal rate, you will take between 12–20 breaths every minute. Every time that you inhale, your lungs fill with air and expand. But you will not feel your lungs beneath your skin, as they are protected by a complex frame of bones that forms your ribcage.

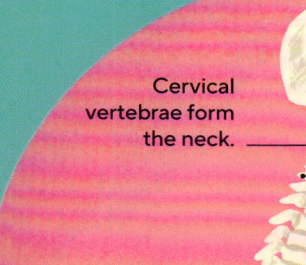

The spine

- Cervical vertebrae form the neck.
- The spine is made up of 33 vertebrae stacked on top of each other, with some fused together.
- A section of lumbar vertebrae at the small of your back supports most of your body's weight.
- The spine curves to form a flexible "S" shape, which allows it to absorb shock when you move.

Why are you taller in the morning than in the evening?

During the day, you spend a lot of time standing up. Gravity pushes on the cartilage discs in your spine, making them lose water. This compresses the spine so that you become ever so slightly shorter. When you lie down horizontally to sleep, the discs rehydrate and swell up again, making you fractionally taller by the time you wake up the following day!

HOW DO YOU SIT UP STRAIGHT?

From your head to your pelvis, a long straight spine snakes down the back of your body. It is made of lots of individual bones called vertebrae, separated by discs of cartilage. These discs act like a cushion between the bones and can squash slightly, allowing you to flex and bend. As well as providing structural support for your body, the spine also protects a thick bundle of nerves called the spinal cord, which carries messages to and from your brain.

Vertebrae in the spine

- Each vertebra has a spur of bone on the back that connects to another.
- Spinal nerves emerge between the vertebrae.
- Discs of cartilage between vertebrae stop them grinding together.

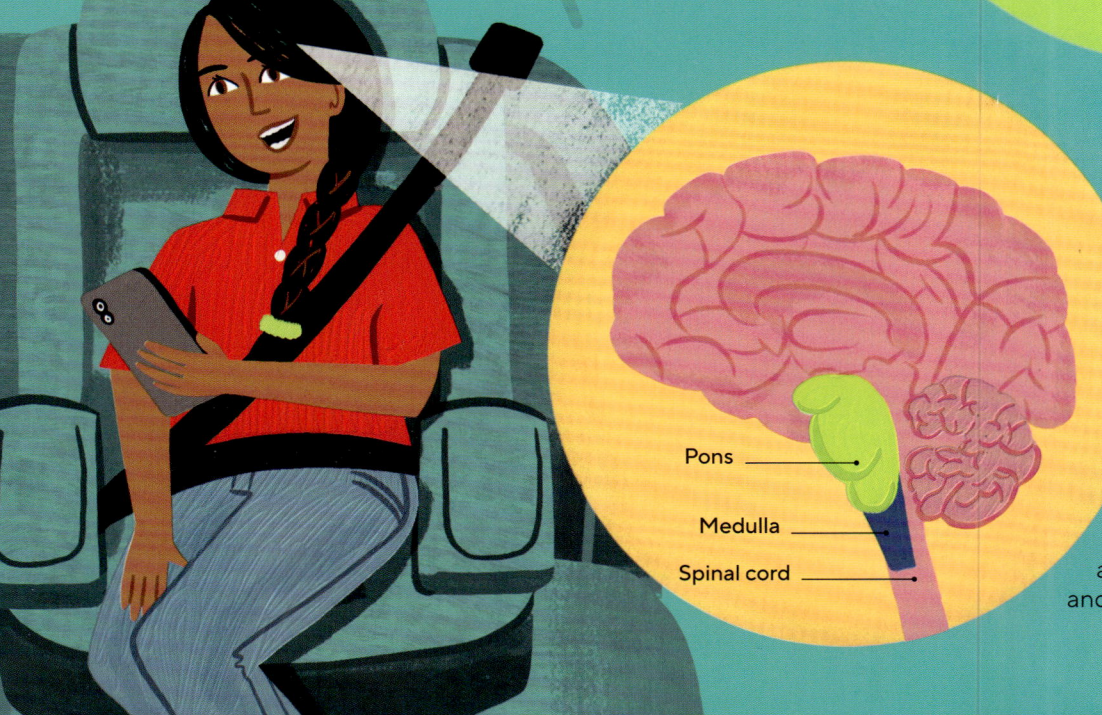

- Pons
- Medulla
- Spinal cord

HOW DO YOU BREATHE AUTOMATICALLY?

Breathing is one of the many processes you do not have to think about, as it is controlled by your central nervous system (your brain and your spinal cord). Where your spinal cord meets the bottom of your brain, there is a part called the brainstem. Inside this, areas known as the pons and medulla send signals to the muscles in your chest and abdomen, telling them to contract and relax at regular intervals.

THE BODY UP HIGH

Freezing temperatures, dazzling sunlight reflecting off ice, and brutal winds all batter the body at high altitude, but by far the greatest challenge is the lack of oxygen. As you climb up from sea level, the oxygen in the air decreases, and each breath pulls in less of this essential gas, making every bodily function a struggle. It can even cause a condition called altitude sickness.

CLIMBING WITHOUT **OXYGEN** BECOMES DANGEROUS AT 7,000 M (23,000 FT) ABOVE **SEA LEVEL**.

LACK OF OXYGEN CAN CAUSE **BLOOD VESSELS** IN THE **LUNGS** TO **NARROW**. THIS CAN **PUSH FLUID** INTO THE LUNGS, MAKING BREATHING TOUGHER.

WHEN IT IS VERY COLD, THE BODY MAY **LOSE** MORE HEAT THAN IT PRODUCES. THIS CAUSES **HYPOTHERMIA**, WHICH PREVENTS ORGANS FROM FUNCTIONING NORMALLY.

ALTITUDE SICKNESS CAUSES DIZZINESS, HEADACHES, SLEEPLESSNESS, AND EVENTUALLY **UNCONSCIOUSNESS**.

HOP, SKIP, AND JUMP

Spending time outside is even more fun when there are playground games. Thankfully, your swinging, skipping body is well supported by a strong skeleton.

WHY DOES IT HURT WHEN YOU HIT YOUR "FUNNY" BONE?

When you knock your elbow in a specific spot, some may say you have hit your "funny bone". However, this unusual sensation is caused by a nerve – not a bone. The ulnar nerve, which runs from your shoulder to your fingers, is squished tight between the skin and bone at your elbow. When you hit it, the nerve is compressed against the bone, causing a sharp, tingling pain.

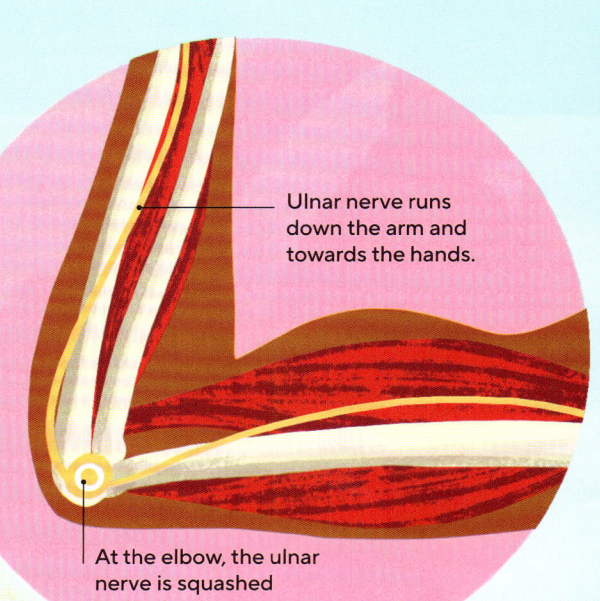

Ulnar nerve runs down the arm and towards the hands.

At the elbow, the ulnar nerve is squashed by the bone.

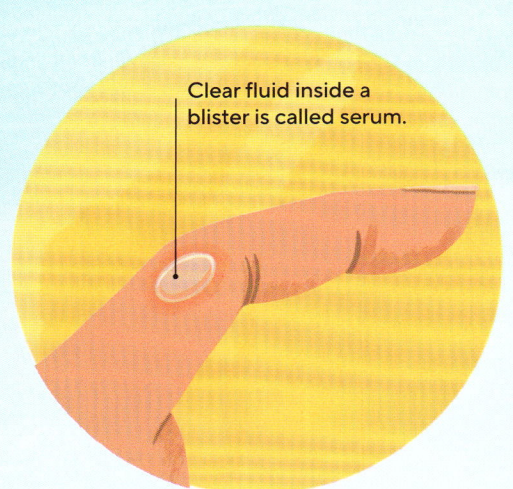

Clear fluid inside a blister is called serum.

WHY DO YOU GET BLISTERS?

Blisters are fluid-filled bubbles. They are caused by friction on the skin, for example when you rub your hands on a rope. This makes the first two layers of skin separate. Fluid then fills the gap in between, creating a protective barrier that allows the skin underneath to heal.

Ribcage protects vital organs – the heart and lungs.

Humerus helps you lift your arm and grab the next bar.

Pelvis transfers body weight from the spine to the legs.

Spine gives the body structure and helps you sit, stand, and bend.

Thigh bone, or the femur, is the longest bone in the human body.

Tibia supports the body's weight when you stand up.

Why do you get static shocks?

Static shocks are caused by the movement of tiny particles you cannot see. These have an electric charge and can build up on your body, for example when you rub your feet on a carpet. If you then touch something made of metal, such as a doorknob, the particles are attracted to this and quickly jump off your body – giving you a zap!

WHAT KEEPS YOUR BODY UPRIGHT?

The skeleton plays an important role in supporting your body – without it, and the muscles that pull on it, you would not be able to stand up straight! Adults have 206 bones, which are divided into two main groups. The axial skeleton (in yellow) is the body's central axis and protects your organs, while the appendicular skeleton (in blue) is made of the body's limbs, which allow you to move.

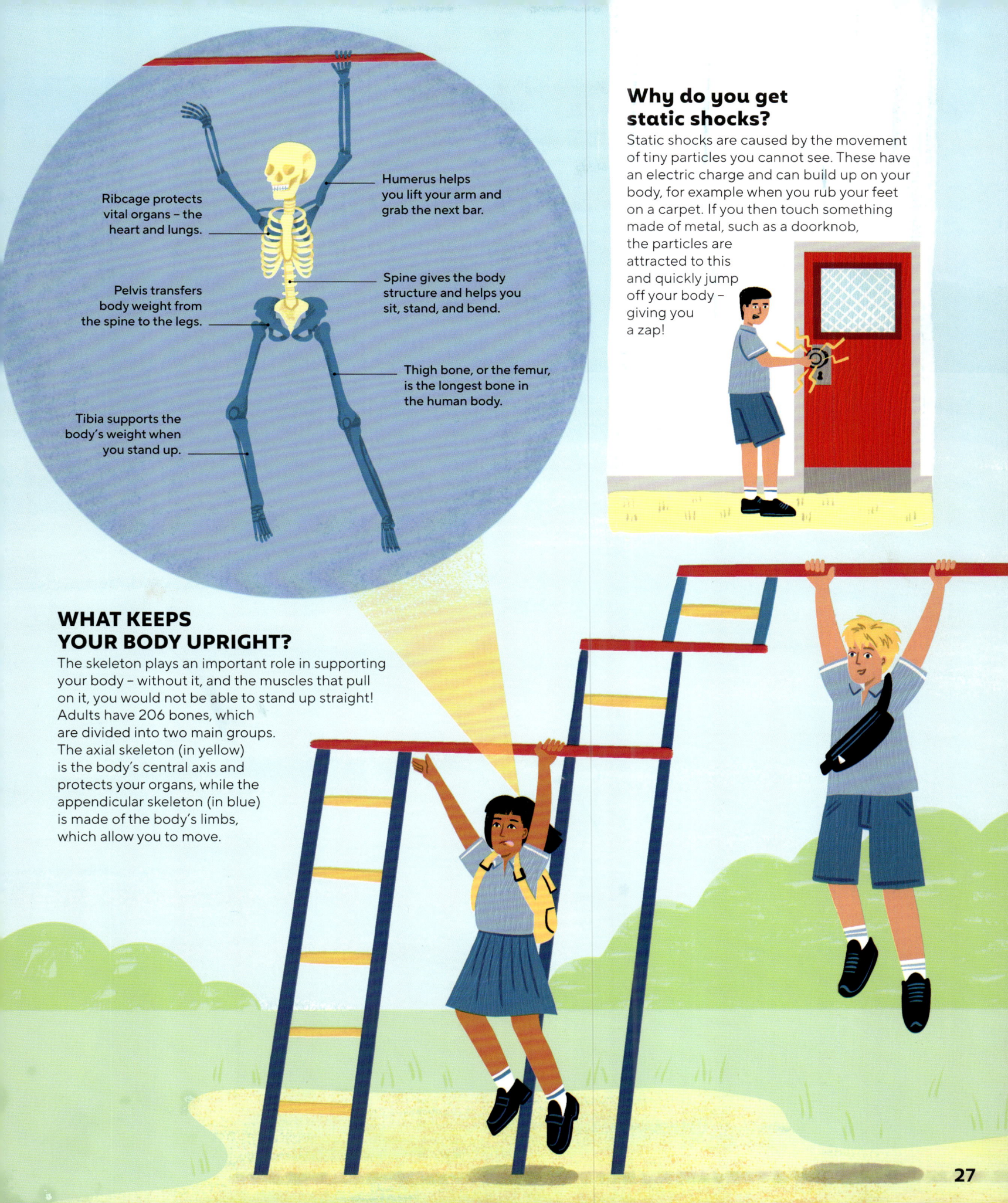

27

BREAKFAST CLUB

The first meal of the day is even more enjoyable with friends. It helps to set you up for whatever the day may bring – from nosebleeds to headaches!

WHY DO YOU GET HEADACHES?

Although it may feel as though a headache is a pain in your head, in fact, your brain cannot feel pain. Instead, special pain receptors in other parts of the body send signals to your brain, and these create the feeling of pain. The aching sensation comes from pain receptors in nerves, such as those in your face and neck.

Nerves across the face transmit signals to the brain about pain.

Nerves in the head

Why is it important to eat breakfast?

Eating a meal in the morning boosts your energy and concentration levels. For a balanced breakfast with a variety of nutrients, try to include foods from different food groups. For example, porridge with milk is a source of carbohydrates and dairy, and eggs have protein. You could add in a fruit, such as a banana, for fibre and a healthy fat, such as an avocado.

Inside a bone

Hard, dense outer layer is called compact bone.

Spongy bone is lightweight but provides strength.

Blood vessels supply oxygen and nutrients.

Red bone marrow fills the gaps in the spongy bone.

Yellow bone marrow is soft and jelly-like in texture.

WHERE DOES BLOOD COME FROM?

Blood is pumped through every part of your body, but it is made in your bones. Throughout your bones is a soft, spongy tissue called bone marrow. Found at the centre of the bone, yellow bone marrow stores fat. But red bone marrow, found towards the end of the bone, produces many of the different components that make up your blood, such as red and white blood cells, and releases them into your bloodstream.

WHY DO YOU GET NOSEBLEEDS?

Although it can feel alarming, bleeding from the nose is actually very common. It happens when the network of delicate blood vessels in the tissues of your nose become damaged, for example, when you blow your nose too hard. Nosebleeds usually only last for up to 15 minutes and the blood vessels inside can heal on their own.

Inside the nose

1. Tissues in the nasal cavity become damaged when your blow your nose.

2. Blood from damaged blood vessels in the tissue leaks through the nostrils.

SNOW DAY

It's not only hats, scarves, and gloves that will protect you from a wintry chill. When your muscles shiver, they are stealthily warming you up.

HOW DOES THE BRAIN KNOW YOU ARE TOO COLD?

The average person has a body temperature of around 37°C (98.6°F). When you get cold, a part of the brain called the hypothalamus receives signals from special cells throughout the body. The hypothalamus then sends signals to other parts of the body to help warm you up.

The hypothalamus monitors body temperature.

Under the skin

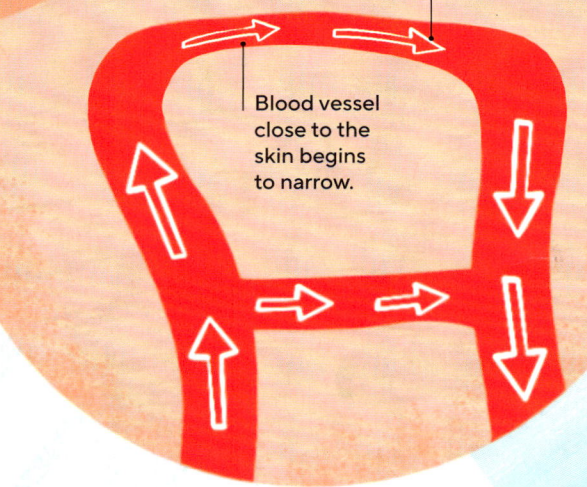

As blood flow reduces, less heat is lost.

Blood vessel close to the skin begins to narrow.

WHY DO YOUR HANDS CHANGE COLOUR WHEN YOU GET COLD?

Many blood vessels sit just under the skin. When you feel cold, the blood vessels in your hands narrow. This reduces the amount of warm blood flowing to the surface of your body, so less heat is lost. Sometimes, the reduced blood flow can make your hands paler.

WHY DO YOU GET GOOSEBUMPS?

Every hair on your body is attached to a muscle. When you are cold, nerves in your body send signals to these muscles and they contract. This muscle movement creates a "bump" which, together with the hair, traps a layer of air near the skin, which helps keep you warm.

Skin hairs

An arrector pili muscle, which is attached to each hair, is relaxed when you are warm.

When you are cold, the muscle contracts and pulls on the hair.

The skin bunches up as the hair stands upright.

WHY DO YOUR TEETH CHATTER TOGETHER?

Shivering is an automatic response when you feel cold. It happens when your skeletal muscles (those attached to your bones) continually tense and relax in quick bursts to generate heat and warm you up. Teeth chattering is a form of shivering where muscles in the jaw rapidly move, making your teeth bash together.

ON THE MOVE
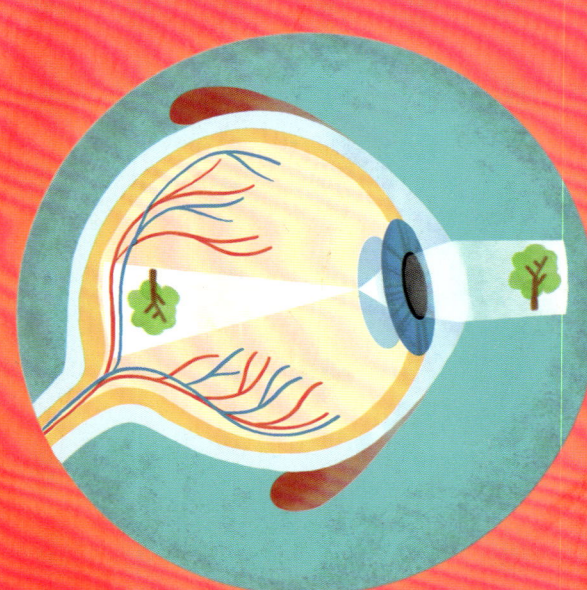

ON THE RUN

A morning jog during P.E. might start out as fun, but it will soon get your heart racing and your lungs burning. Afterwards, you might feel tired, happy, or both!

WHY DO YOU GET OUT OF BREATH?

Every time you breathe in, a muscle called the diaphragm contracts, drawing in air. This contains oyxgen – vital fuel for your cells. Running works your body hard, so it needs more oxygen, causing you to breathe faster and feel out of breath.

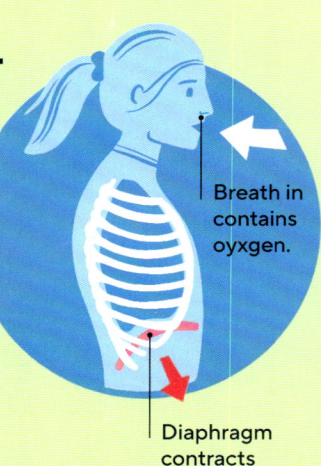

Breath in contains oyxgen.

Breath out contains waste gas carbon dioxide.

Diaphragm contracts

Diaphragm relaxes

WHY DOES YOUR HEART BEAT FASTER?

The heart pumps blood around your body, which carries the oxygen from your lungs to your muscles. Each time it pumps, you feel it as a heart beat. To keep up with the supply demanded by your rapidly moving leg muscles, it begins to pump at a faster rate.

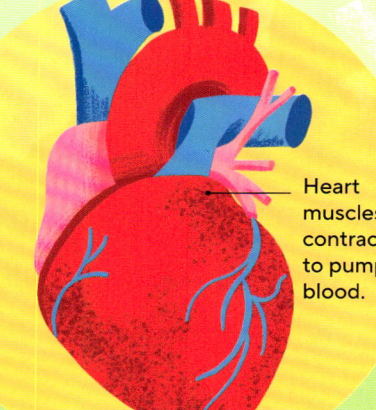

Heart muscles contract to pump blood.

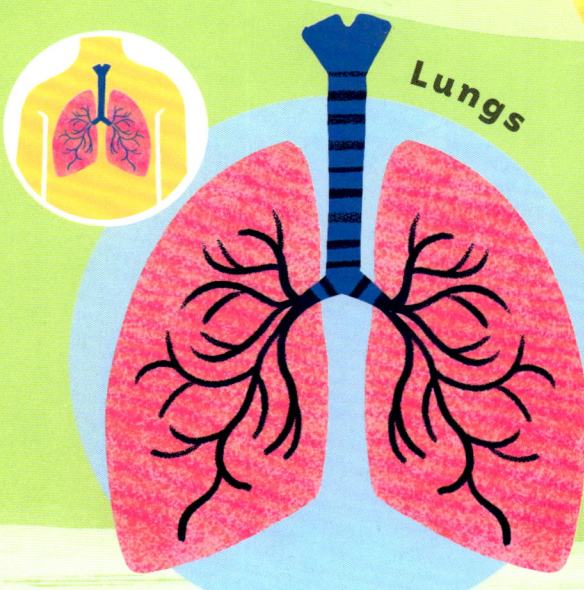

Lungs

WHAT DO YOUR LUNGS DO?

Your lungs are large sacs that expand as you draw in air and relax when you breathe out. Inside, they are filled with lots of little branching tubes. Oxygen from the air is channelled through these tubes and passed into the bloodstream (see pages 22–23).

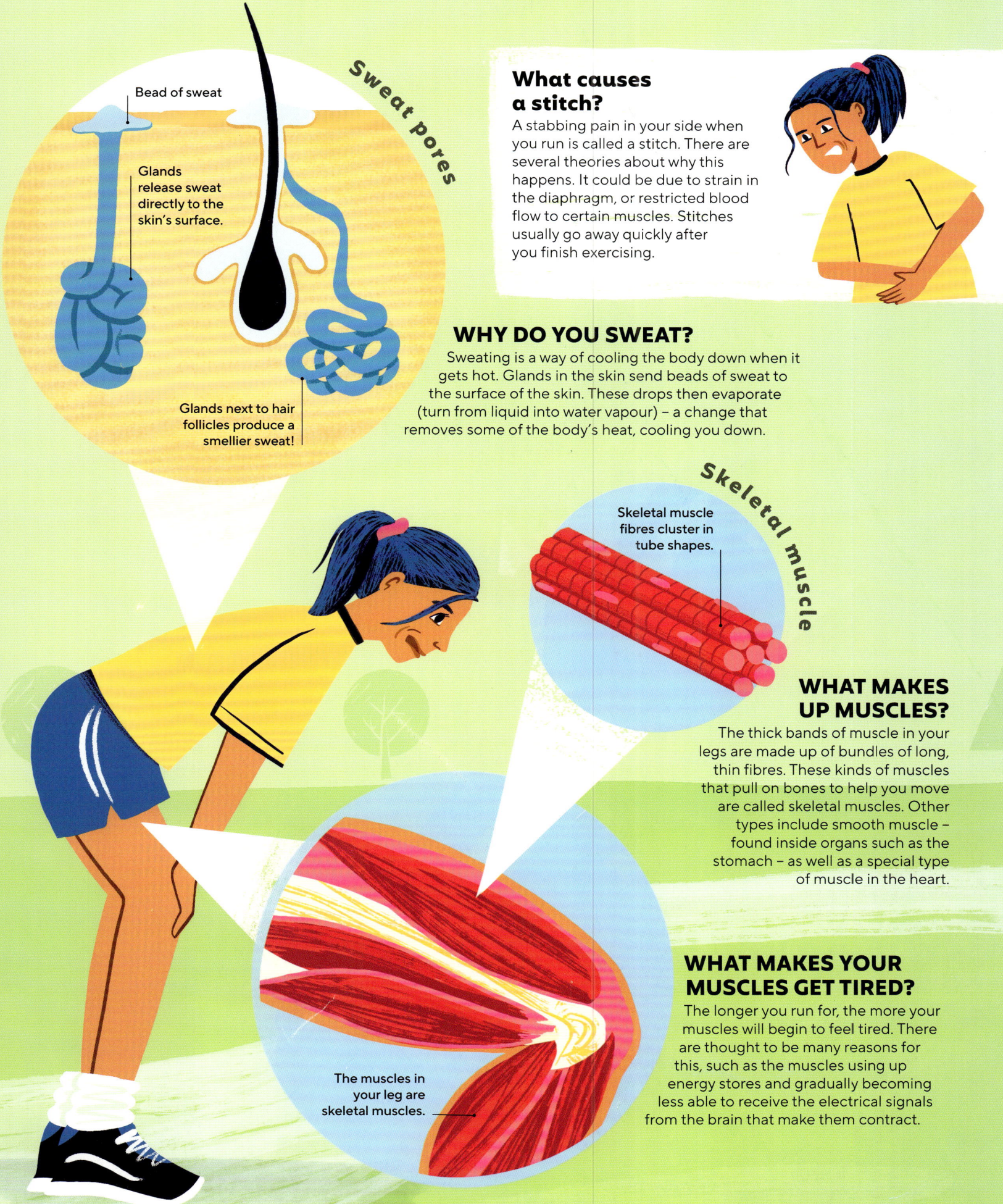

THIRSTY WORK

Taking a trip to the water fountain might feel needed after exercising or eating a salty snack. But your body constantly needs water whatever you are doing.

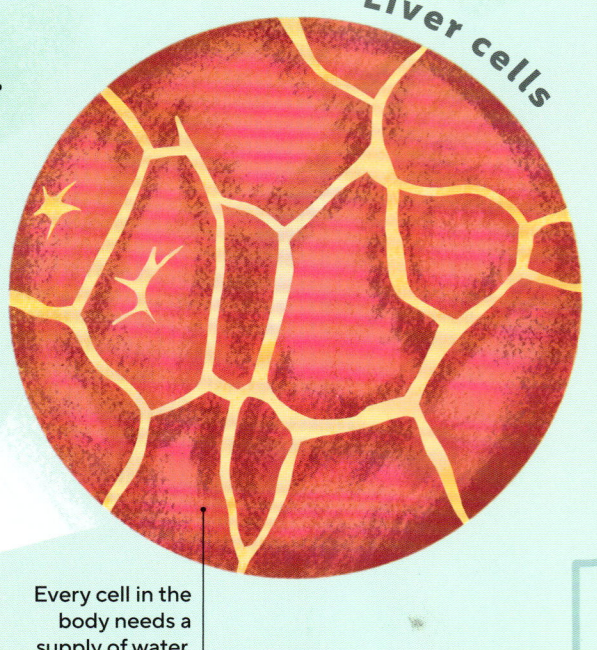

Liver cells

WHY DO YOU NEED WATER?

When you drink water, it gets absorbed into the body and sent to all your cells, including those that make up major organs such as the liver. These cells need water to carry out the processes that generate energy. Your brain carefully regulates how much water moves in and out of your body as you drink, sweat, and wee to ensure the balance of water is always at the right level.

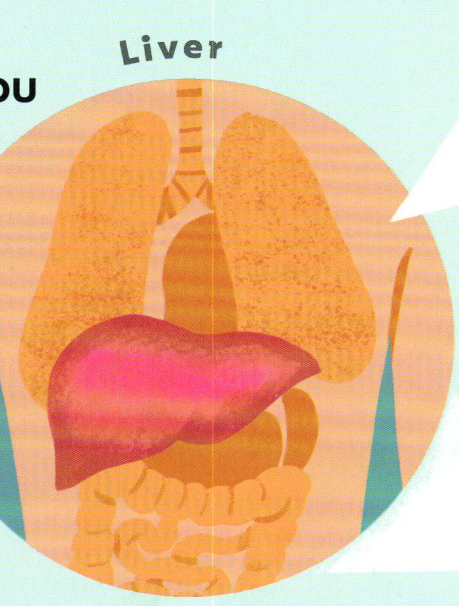

Liver

Every cell in the body needs a supply of water.

HOW MUCH WATER IS INSIDE YOU?

Between 55 and 60 per cent of an adult's body is water. Children have a slightly higher percentage, and newborn babies are made up of 74 per cent water! This might sound like a lot, but water helps to make up all our major organs, such as the brain, and is the main part of our blood.

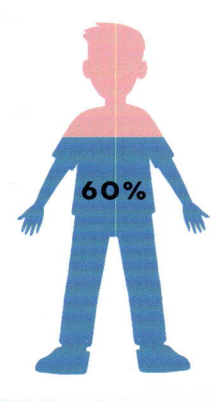

60%

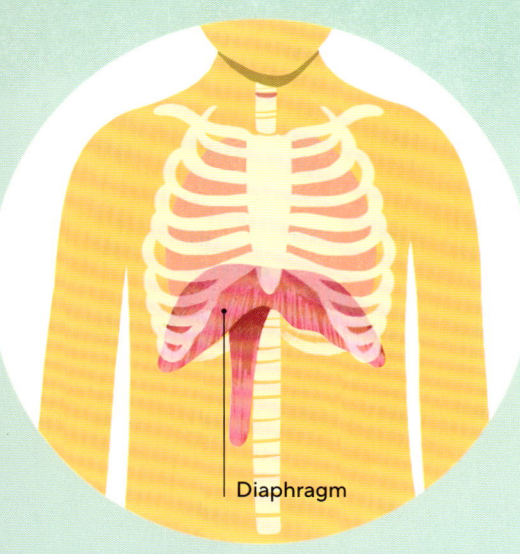
Diaphragm

WHY DO YOU GET A DRY MOUTH WHEN YOU ARE THIRSTY?

When you need more water, a part of the brain called the hypothalamus sends a trigger to produce the feeling of being thirsty. Less fluid in the body may also mean less saliva is produced. As you drink, your brain anticipates feeling hydrated even before the water has been absorbed and stops making you feel thirsty in advance.

1. The hypothalamus recognizes low levels of water in the body, and makes you feel thirsty.

2. As water enters the body, signals are sent back to the brain.

WHY DO YOU GET HICCUPS?

When you breathe in, a muscle called your diaphragm contracts to help your lungs take in air. However, sometimes your diaphragm moves irregularly, in spasms, only drawing in little bits of air. This can be caused by many factors, such as eating too much too fast. When this happens, the little pockets of air slap against your vocal cords – producing that funny hic sound!

How much water should you drink?

Everybody is different, but experts recommend that the average child should drink around six to eight glasses of water every day. If you are exercising a lot or the weather is hot, you will need to drink more. It is best to keep drinking regularly and not to wait until you're really thirsty.

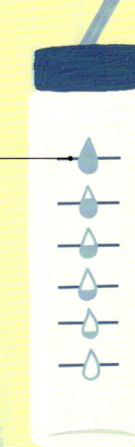

A full 1-litre (1.7-pint) water bottle contains just over half the water you need in a day.

QUEASY RIDE

Long bus journeys are no fun when you feel sick. The dizziness and nausea are your body's response to mismatched signals from your eyes and ears.

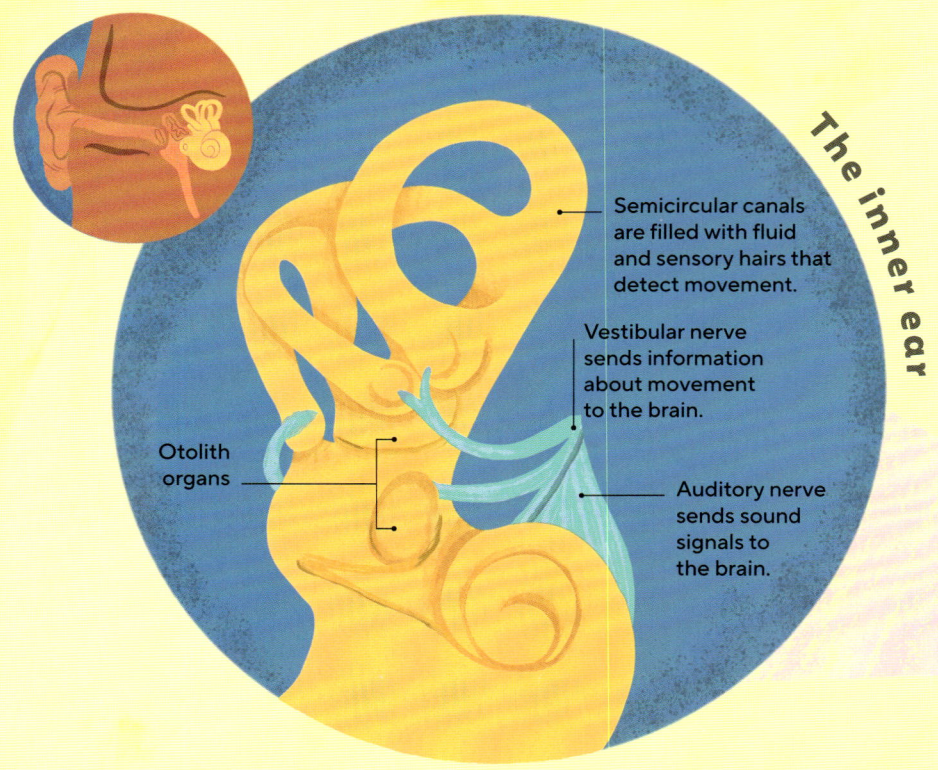

The inner ear

- Semicircular canals are filled with fluid and sensory hairs that detect movement.
- Vestibular nerve sends information about movement to the brain.
- Otolith organs
- Auditory nerve sends sound signals to the brain.

HOW DOES YOUR BRAIN KNOW WHEN YOU ARE MOVING?

Inside your inner ear (see page 66) are small looped tubes called semicircular canals. Together with structures called the otolith organs, they detect when and how your body moves, such as whether you are rotating your head or running forwards. This sensory information is then fed back to the brain, which tells your body how to keep balanced.

Can virtual reality make you feel sick?

Using virtual reality headsets can make some people feel queasy. The immersive headset blocks out the real world and makes your brain think that you are moving, even if you are standing still. This confusing information can make you feel sick!

38

How sight works

1. Light from an object enters the eye.
2. Light ray bends as it enters the eye.
3. A lens focuses light rays onto the retina.
4. Upside-down image forms on the retina.
5. Optic nerve sends signals to the brain, where the image is turned the right way up.

Pupil

WHY DO YOU FEEL SICK ON THE BUS?

If your brain receives conflicting information from your eyes and ears, you may feel nauseous. This is what happens on the bus if you focus on a stationary object, such as the seat in front of you or a book, rather than look out of the window. Your eyes signal to the brain that you are sitting still, but at the same time the organs in your ears are detecting the movement of the bus. Your brain is unsure if you are moving or not!

Feeling queasy

1. You feel queasy as the intestines push food back up the digestive system.
2. Food reenters the stomach, which begins to fill up.

Vomiting

3. Stomach is squeezed as the abdominal walls contract when retching.
4. Food is forced up into the oesophagus and out of your throat in a sudden wave.

WHAT MAKES YOU VOMIT?

Eating spoiled food, stomach bugs, and motion sickness are all reasons why you might vomit. The brain controls the physical act of being sick by sending signals to the digestive tract. The smooth muscle that lines the intestines and stomach then begins to contract, moving food upwards until it is expelled from your mouth.

39

THE BODY IN SPACE

Humans are not built for life in space! Even the shortest mission can have a dramatic impact on the body. One of the main challenges is microgravity – the lack of downward gravitational pull. This affects virtually all the body's systems. On spacewalks, a spacesuit provides essential life support: without it, a human would lose consciousness in just 15 seconds!

MUSCLES WASTE AWAY IN MICROGRAVITY. ASTRONAUTS CAN LOSE UP TO 40% OF THEIR **MUSCLE MASS** IN JUST THREE MONTHS.

BONES BECOME MORE FRAGILE IN SPACE, **LOSING UP TO 1.5%** OF THEIR DENSITY EVERY MONTH.

IN MICROGRAVITY, **FLUIDS IN THE BODY** MOVE UPWARDS, GIVING ASTRONAUTS THINNER-LOOKING **LEGS AND A PUFFED-UP FACE!**

SCIENTISTS HAVE FOUND THAT THE **EPIDERMIS LAYER OF SKIN** GETS THINNER BY NEARLY 20% AFTER SIX MONTHS IN SPACE.

YOU CAN'T SHOWER IN SPACE. ASTRONAUTS MAINTAIN **CLEAN, GERM-FREE BODIES** WITH DAILY SPONGE-DOWNS.

MICROGRAVITY IN SPACE ALLOWS THE **SPINE TO STRETCH OUT**. ASTRONAUTS CAN GROW UP TO 5 CM (2 IN) TALLER!

WOULD-BE ASTRONAUTS **TRAIN IN WATER AND LOW GRAVITY SIMULATORS** TO IMPROVE THEIR FITNESS BEFORE THEY GO TO SPACE.

ON THE INTERNATIONAL SPACE STATION, THE **SUN RISES AND SETS EVERY 90 MINUTES**. EARPLUGS AND EYE MASKS HELP ASTRONAUTS KEEP TO THEIR NORMAL SLEEP CYCLES.

THE **LONGEST TIME** ANY ASTRONAUT HAS SPENT CONTINUOUSLY IN SPACE IS **437 DAYS**.

SPACE FOOD IS OFTEN MORE SPICY THAN ON EARTH, BECAUSE **TASTE BUDS LOSE THEIR SENSITIVITY**.

ART ATTACK

An art lesson allows you to flex your fingers and prepare to paint! Many different parts of your body need to work together to produce each colourful creation.

HOW DO YOU GRIP A PAINTBRUSH?

Your hand is made of lots of tiny bones connected together by joints. Strong tendons pull on the bones to move the hand into different shapes, so that you can hold small objects such as pens or paintbrushes. Unlike lots of other animals, humans have opposable thumbs – a feature where the thumb can move to touch all of the other fingers.

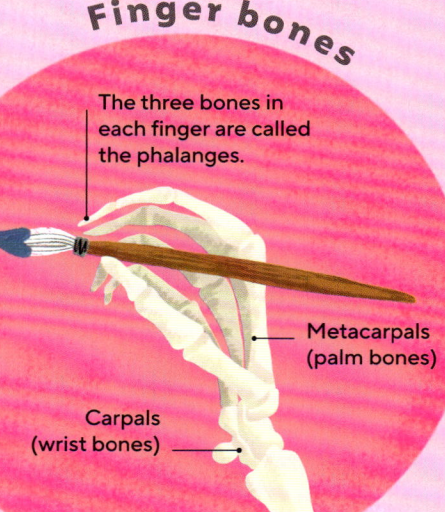

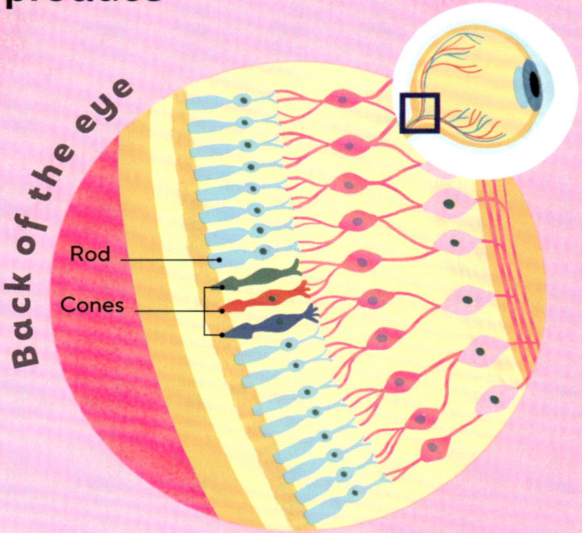

Finger bones

The three bones in each finger are called the phalanges.

Metacarpals (palm bones)

Carpals (wrist bones)

Back of the eye

Rod

Cones

HOW CAN YOU SEE COLOUR?

Special cells at the back of the eye called rods and cones convert light into signals that are sent to the brain. Rods work well in low light, but only pick up details in black and white. Cones pick up colours and more detail.

HOW DO VEINS WORK?

Veins are needed to take blood back to the heart, carrying away waste products such as carbon dioxide. Compared to arteries, veins carry blood at a low pressure and have valves to stop blood flowing backwards after it has passed through. This means the blood can only flow one way.

Open valve

1. When the skeletal muscle contracts, it squashes the vein, making blood flow.

2. Blood flow opens the valve.

3. As the muscle relaxes, the valve closes.

4. Blood is prevented from flowing backwards.

Closed valve

Veins in the arm

Veins in each finger join to form larger veins, which travel up the arm.

WHY DO YOUR VEINS LOOK BLUE OR GREEN?

Depending on your skin colour, you may be able to see blue-green veins snaking beneath the surface of your skin. Due to a trick of the light, these veins can appear blue or green but the blood is still red! Unlike the blood in most arteries, the blood carried in most veins no longer contains oxygen, so is a darker colour.

Why do you feel anxious?

Anxiety is a normal feeling and is your body responding to something it finds scary. Anxiety can be a helpful feeling that can keep you safe and enable you to stay away from hazards, but it can also feel overwhelming and prevent you from doing things.

What are the physical symptoms of anxiety?

Feeling anxious may cause symptoms, such as a faster heartbeat, shortness of breath, and racing thoughts. These reactions happen because your body is getting into "fight or flight mode", ready to face off a threat – even if the threat is small or a false alarm!

FEELING ANXIOUS

School can be stressful and preparing for big moments such as tests might make you feel more nervous than usual. These feelings are a sign that the test is important to you, and that your anxiety is encouraging you to do your best.

What is happening in your brain when you feel anxious?

The brain has several parts for dealing with emotions, but one key area is called the amygdala, which processes fear and anxiety. This interacts with other parts of your brain and triggers the release of hormones around the body, causing the physical changes you experience.

Is it normal to feel worried all the time?

Everyone gets worried – whether it is about making new friends or doing well on schoolwork – but if you find yourself feeling constantly anxious it is advisable to talk to a teacher, family member, trusted adult, or doctor and find ways to manage this.

Why do you feel worried about doing well at school?

Tests, speaking in front of people, and even homework deadlines are all very common situations that cause people to feel anxiety. Because these things feel important, they can make you imagine and worry about the worst possible scenario.

How can I feel less anxious?

 Speak to friends and family and share your worries. You might feel reassured that others have similar worries too!

 Take deep breaths. Breathe in for four seconds and breathe out for six to eight seconds.

 Notice what makes your anxiety more intense and find something that calms you down instead.

TOILET TIME

What goes in must come out! But the waste that plops into the toilet has taken a long route through your body, changing along the way.

HOW DOES POO FORM?
When food has passed through the small intestine, it ends up as chyme – a mixture of partially digested food and gastric juices. It then travels through the large lumpy tube of the large intestine, where water and all leftover nutrients are absorbed. This leaves just waste, which forms poo.

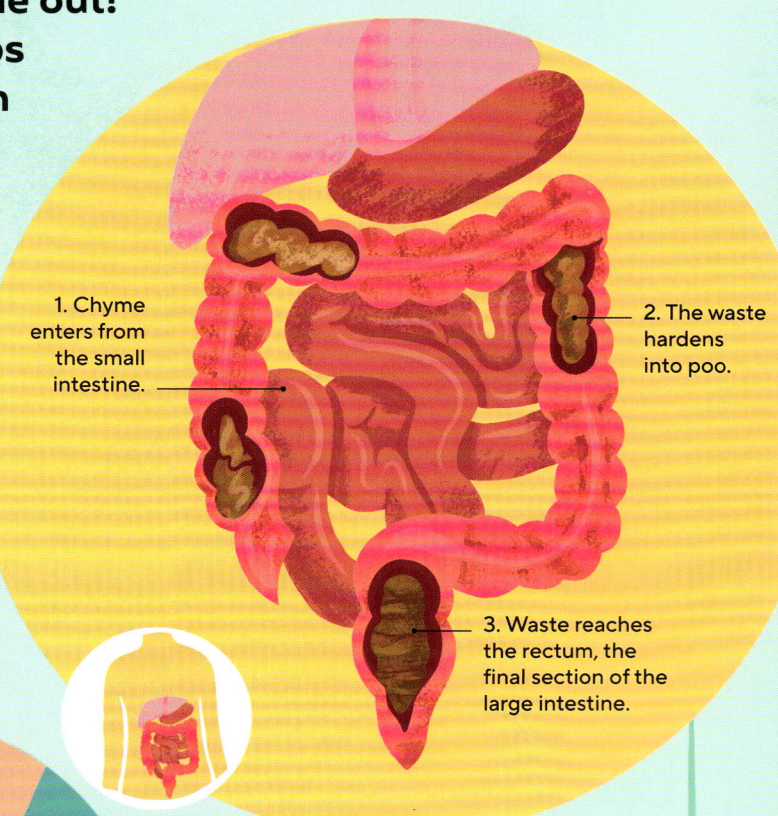

1. Chyme enters from the small intestine.
2. The waste hardens into poo.
3. Waste reaches the rectum, the final section of the large intestine.

HOW LONG DOES FOOD TAKE TO PASS THROUGH YOU?
It can take from one to three days for food to pass the full length of the digestive system. This varies from person to person depending on their metabolism – how fast the processes happen that turn food and drink into energy for cells. A butterfly-shaped gland in your neck called the thyroid helps to control the metabolism by releasing different hormones.

Thyroid gland

Why do some foods, such as sweetcorn, show up in your poo?
The outer layer of a sweetcorn kernel is made up of a rubbery substance called cellulose. This does not break apart easily when chewed, so the body digests the inside of the corn and expels the skin. Nuts and seeds and other foods high in fibre (which therefore aren't fully digested) can also appear in poo.

WHY DOESN'T POO ALWAYS LOOK THE SAME?

The consistency of your poo (how hard or runny it is) can change over days and weeks depending on many factors, such as what you have eaten and whether you are unwell. Doctors use the Bristol stool chart to measure the types of poo humans produce. There are seven different types, with an ideal poo being somewhere in the middle.

Type 1
Small, hard lumps of poo that are hard to pass suggest you may be constipated (find it hard to pass poo).

Type 4
A long, smooth piece of poo that comes out easily is the best way to expel waste!

Type 7
Completely runny poo is often called diarrhoea and can indicate that you are not well.

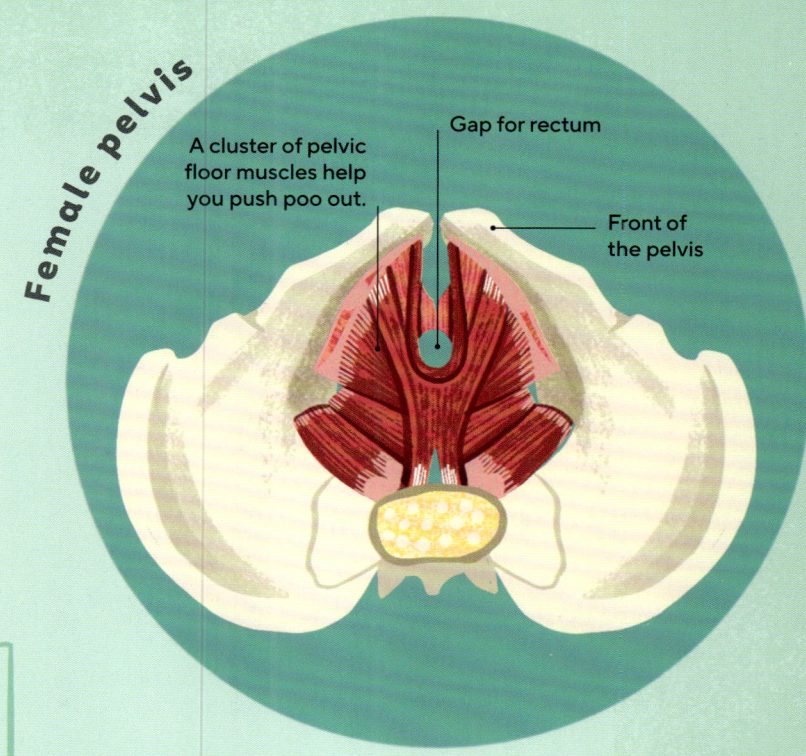

Female pelvis

- A cluster of pelvic floor muscles help you push poo out.
- Gap for rectum
- Front of the pelvis

WHY DO YOU HAVE TO PUSH POO OUT?

To release poo from your body, you relax your outer sphincter muscle. But sometimes it can be tougher to push poo out. Other muscles in the body, such as those in your pelvis (known as the pelvic floor muscles) and those in your belly (known as abdominals), can be squeezed or tensed to put pressure on your rectum and help release poo.

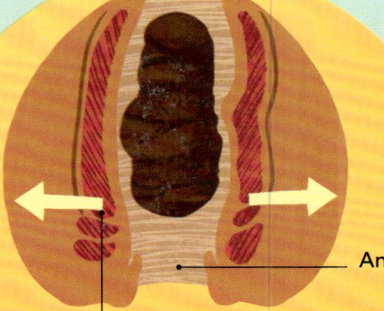

Internal sphincter muscles relax, allowing poo to travel into the anus.

Anus

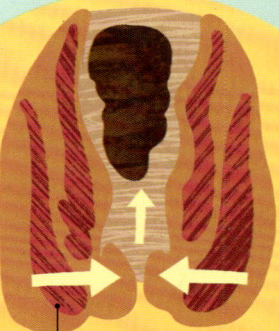

External sphincter muscles squeeze, preventing poo from leaving the body.

WHAT MAKES YOU NEED TO POO?

When enough poo accumulates in the rectum (the final part of your intestine), it stretches the walls. This sends signals to the brain, which opens a ring of muscle called the inner sphincter and lets the poo down into your anus. If you are not near a toilet, you can squeeze the muscles of the outer sphincter to push the poo back in.

LEAP AND TWIST

A gymnastics move is no easy feat. To build up your muscles and flexibility, you'll need plenty of practice, patience, and body strength!

WHY ARE SOME PEOPLE SO FLEXIBLE?

Anyone can improve their flexibility with regular stretching. But people who are naturally more flexible than others have joint hypermobility. They are often called double-jointed, but they do not have unusual joints. Their ligaments – tough bands of tissue that connect two bones together – are just very stretchy, giving their joints a wider range of movement.

Muscle
Tendon
Bone
Ligament

Leg muscles

Hamstring muscles bend the knee joint.

Quadriceps muscles straighten the knee joint.

Calf muscles are used to flex the foot and jump.

Peroneal muscles help turn the foot outwards.

HOW DO YOUR LEG MUSCLES GET STRONGER?

There are lots of muscles in your legs, and when you exercise, you create microscopic tears in the muscle fibres. Your body then repairs these fibres, giving you bigger and stronger muscles. The more that you work your leg muscles, the stronger they will get.

48

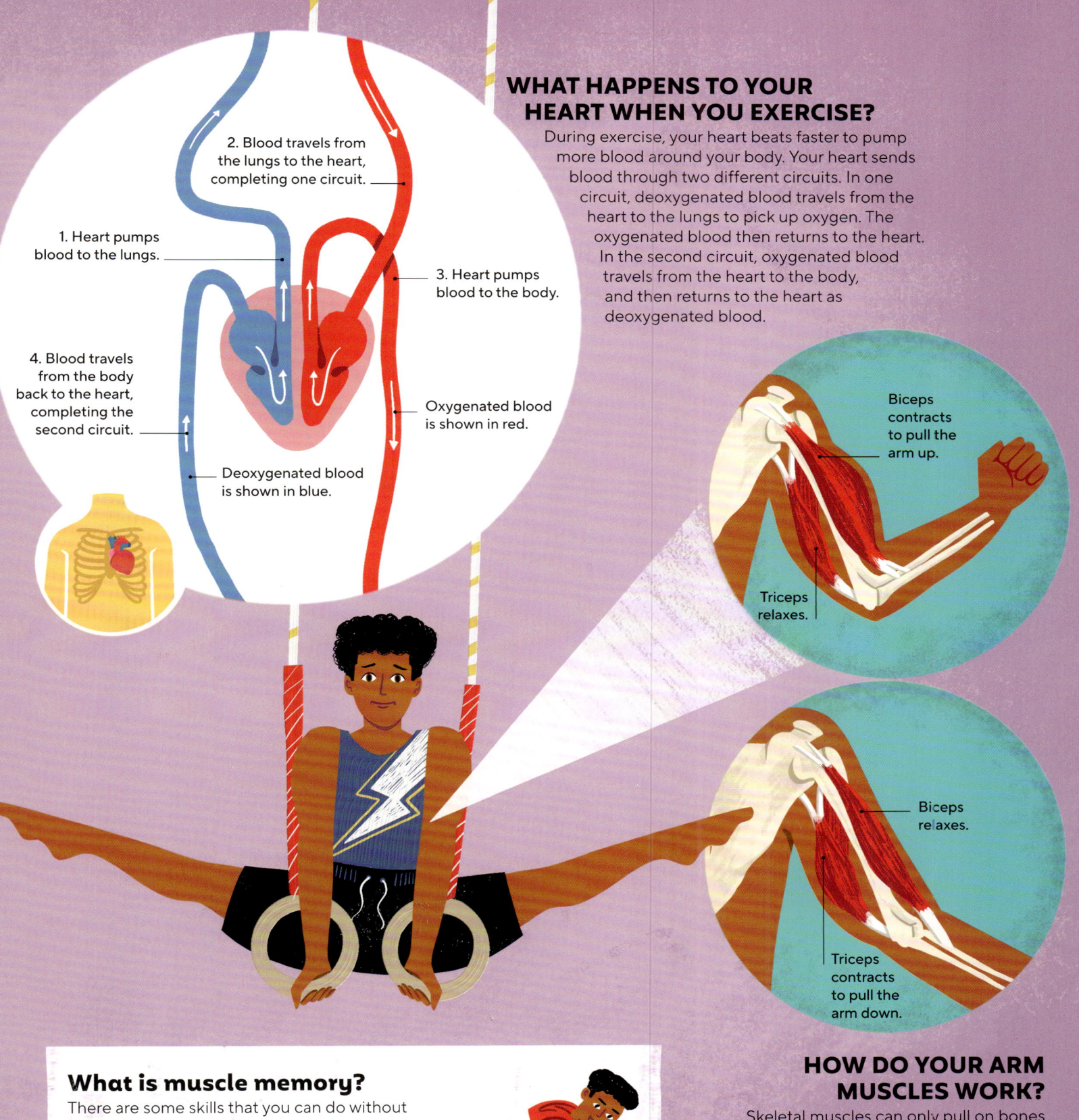

WHAT HAPPENS TO YOUR HEART WHEN YOU EXERCISE?

During exercise, your heart beats faster to pump more blood around your body. Your heart sends blood through two different circuits. In one circuit, deoxygenated blood travels from the heart to the lungs to pick up oxygen. The oxygenated blood then returns to the heart. In the second circuit, oxygenated blood travels from the heart to the body, and then returns to the heart as deoxygenated blood.

1. Heart pumps blood to the lungs.
2. Blood travels from the lungs to the heart, completing one circuit.
3. Heart pumps blood to the body.
4. Blood travels from the body back to the heart, completing the second circuit.

Oxygenated blood is shown in red.
Deoxygenated blood is shown in blue.

Biceps contracts to pull the arm up.
Triceps relaxes.

Biceps relaxes.
Triceps contracts to pull the arm down.

HOW DO YOUR ARM MUSCLES WORK?

Skeletal muscles can only pull on bones (they cannot push) and work together in pairs. To curl your arm, your biceps muscle contracts, pulling your arm inwards, and your triceps muscle relaxes. To straighten your arm, the opposite happens – your triceps contracts and your biceps relaxes.

What is muscle memory?

There are some skills that you can do without thinking, such as tying your shoes. This is called muscle memory. When you first learn a skill, connections are made between nerve cells in the brain, allowing signals to move through a specific pathway. When you practise, the pathway strengthens as more signals pass through. Eventually, the action becomes automatic.

AT THE DOCTOR'S

Germs be warned – your body has a smart system of defences to protect against illness. But some sicknesses or injuries need to be checked out by a medical professional.

WHAT CAN YOU HEAR THROUGH A STETHOSCOPE?

Inside your chest is a noisy place – air is constantly passing in and out of your lungs and blood is being pumped out by your heart. To check both these organs are working normally, a doctor uses a tool called a stethoscope to listen in. Sound waves travel along the rubber tubes into the doctor's ears. This allows them to spot any unusual wheezing or crackling in the lungs, or irregular heart rhythms.

Air going in and out of the lungs can make lots of different sounds.

Stethoscope chest piece picks up sound waves as vibrations.

Listening to the lungs

Why can being ill make you feel hotter?

When your body temperature rises, it is often a sign that it is fighting germs. The natural temperature inside your body is around 37°C (98.6°F), but when your system detects harmful bacteria or viruses, your brain makes your body temperature rise – making it harder for these invaders to survive.

WHY CAN YOUR NECK FEEL SWOLLEN WHEN YOU ARE ILL?

Many harmful germs get stopped by your body's first barriers, such as your skin and mucus. Any germs that make it past these are stopped by the lymphatic system (see page 131). This network of tubes all over your body collects excess fluid from your body tissues and passes it through small glands called nodes. Inside these, white blood cells attack germs and the fluid is cleaned, ready to be returned to the bloodstream. But when you're fighting off an infection, many more white blood cells arrive in the nodes – causing these to swell up in key areas such as the neck and armpits.

Lymph vessels drain and transport excess fluid.

Nodes are where the fluid is cleaned of harmful substances.

Nodes in the neck can swell when more white blood cells are needed.

Lymphatic system in the head

WHY DO YOU GET COLDS?

Viruses can enter through your nose or mouth.

Colds are caused by tiny germs called viruses. They are one of the most common illnesses because they spread so easily. They pass from one person to another, travelling through the air in droplets so tiny you cannot see them and entering your body when you breathe. The symptoms you experience, such as a cough or a runny nose, are your body's way of fighting back against the virus and trying to get rid of it.

Spleen

The spleen is your body's largest lymph organ.

HOW DOES YOUR BODY DEFEND ITSELF AGAINST INFECTIONS?

White blood cells are your body's defence system and destroy germs (see page 61). They are made in an organ called the spleen, which can also remove old or damaged red blood cells.

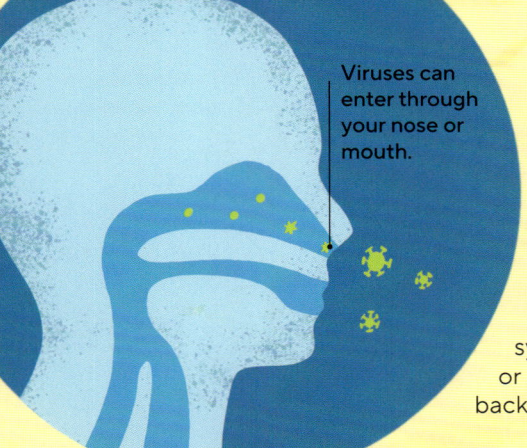

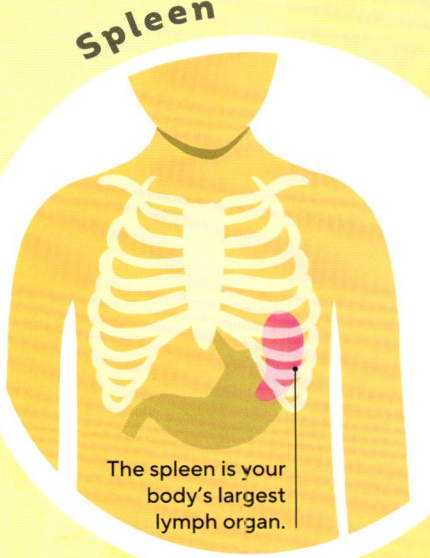

FIRST AID KIT

You don't need to see a doctor for every injury or illness. Kept in schools and the home, items such as plasters and painkillers can be used to treat minor medical problems.

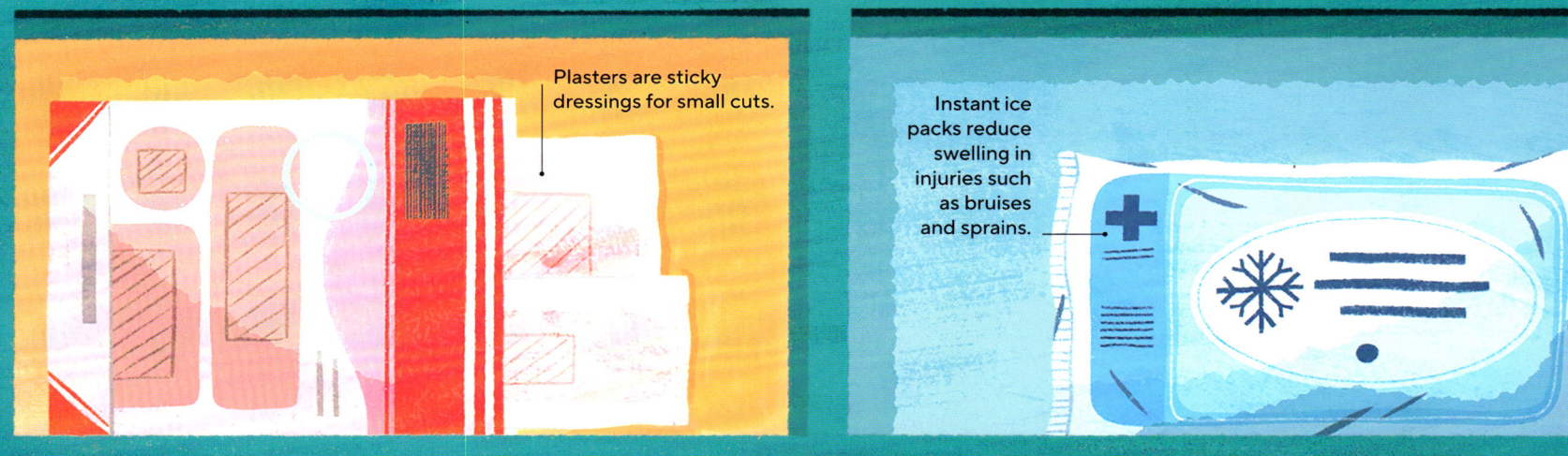

Plasters are sticky dressings for small cuts.

Instant ice packs reduce swelling in injuries such as bruises and sprains.

ANTISEPTIC WIPES

Antiseptic wipes are used to clean and sanitize a small graze, cut, or wound on the skin. They kill germs and bacteria, and help prevent infection. Antiseptic wipes can also be used to disinfect your hands when you do not have access to soap and water to wash them with.

Each wipe is used once and then thrown away to stop germs spreading.

ANTIHISTAMINES

Antihistamine tablets are taken when you have an allergic reaction, such as hayfever. They can help ease allergy symptoms such as a runny nose, sneezing, and itchy eyes. However, some antihistamine tablets may make you feel drowsy, too.

Antihistamines come in many different forms, such as tablets.

PAINKILLERS

Paracetamol and ibuprofen are simple painkillers. They are used for mild to moderate aches and pains, such as headaches and sore muscles, and to help reduce a high temperature. Medicines of any kind should only be taken on the advice of a trusted adult.

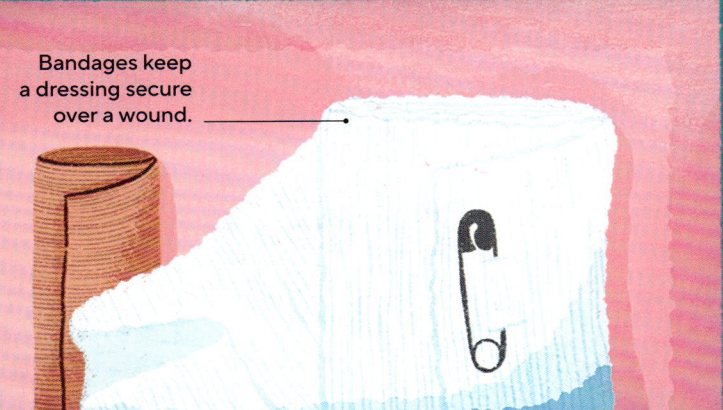

Bandages keep a dressing secure over a wound.

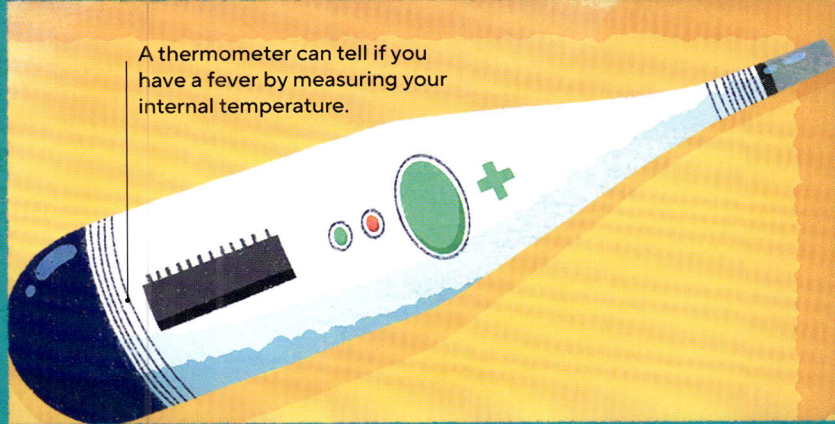

A thermometer can tell if you have a fever by measuring your internal temperature.

VAPOUR RUB

When used on the throat and chest, vapour rub helps temporarily relieve symptoms of congestion, such as a stuffy nose. It contains menthol, which creates a cooling sensation when you breathe it in, making you feel as though you are less congested.

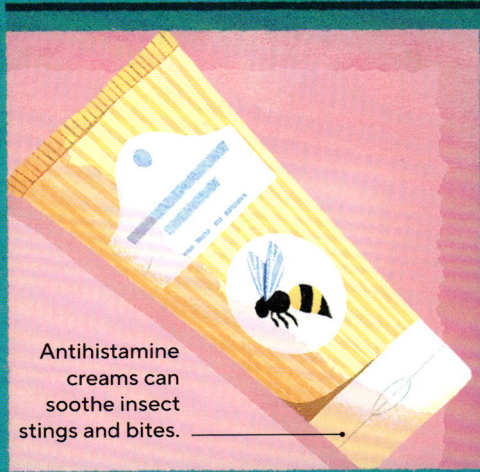

Antihistamine creams can soothe insect stings and bites.

A sun protection factor (SPF) of at least 30 is recommended for children.

SUNSCREEN

Sunscreen protects your skin from the Sun's ultraviolet (UV) rays, which can cause sunburn. It is recommended to use a thick layer of cream when applying over your whole body, and to reapply every two hours. Even while wearing sunscreen, don't stay in the sun for too long!

WORKING HARD

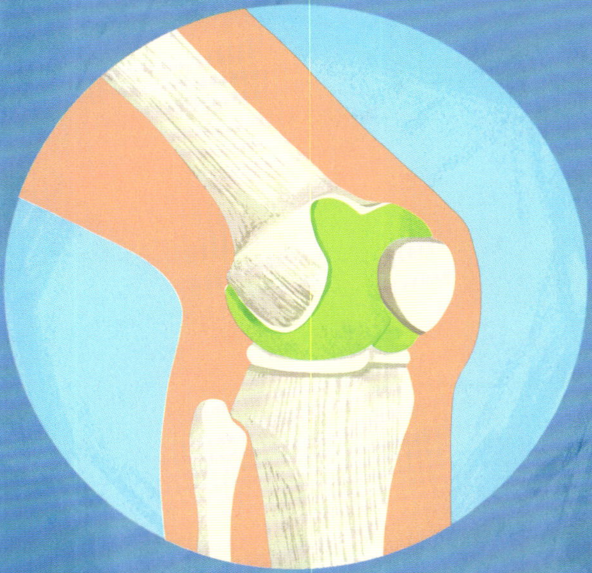

WATCH, LISTEN, AND LEARN

Paying attention at school is hard. Your ears, eyes, and brain must manage masses of new information across multiple subjects.

WHICH PART OF YOUR BRAIN TAKES IN INFORMATION?

Most of the information processing takes place in the cerebral cortex. This is the outermost area of the brain, made up of so many tiny folds that it looks wrinkly. Information received from each of the five senses is processed in a different part of the cerebral cortex.

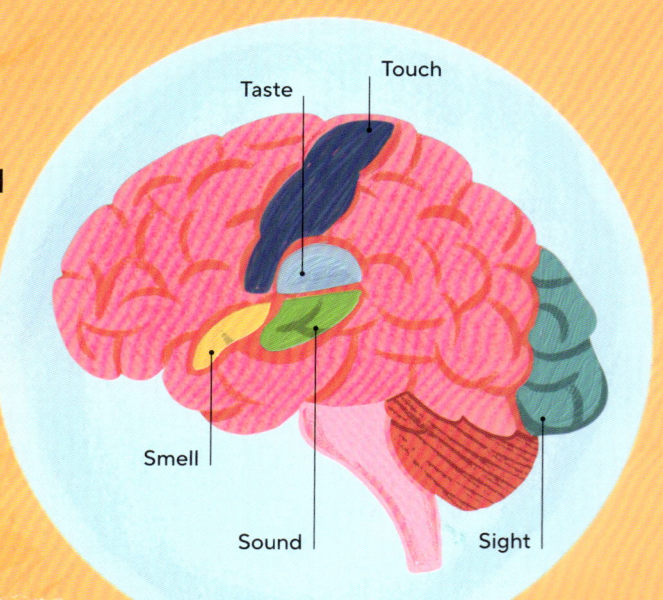

Taste · Touch · Smell · Sound · Sight

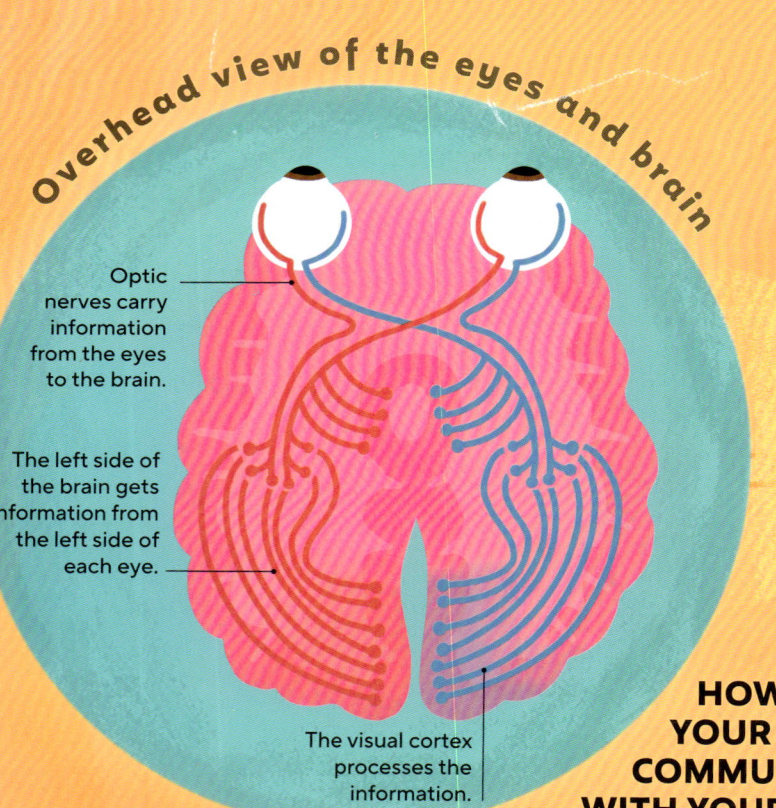

Overhead view of the eyes and brain

- Optic nerves carry information from the eyes to the brain.
- The left side of the brain gets information from the left side of each eye.
- The visual cortex processes the information.

HOW DO YOUR EYES COMMUNICATE WITH YOUR BRAIN?

Light entering your eyes is turned into electrical signals, which are then sent through the optic nerves to reach your brain. Each eye has a slightly different view. The brain combines the information from both eyes to form a 3D image, giving us what is called binocular vision.

HOW CAN YOU TELL WHERE SOUNDS ARE COMING FROM?

The outer part of your ear receives sound waves travelling through the air and funnels them down a channel called the ear canal. To figure out exactly where these sounds came from, the brain compares those that reached the right ear and the left ear to make an estimate.

WHY DO YOU NEED TO BLINK?

Your eyelids work like windscreen wipers on a car – constantly clearing away dust and dirt and washing the surface of the eye with tear fluid. Blinking also sharpens your vision by keeping the surface layer of your eye moist. If you stopped blinking, your eyes would soon dry out!

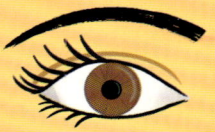

WHY MIGHT YOU SEE LETTERS THE WRONG WAY ROUND?

Letters often look jumbled up to people with dyslexia – a type of neurodivergence, where the brain operates differently to what is seen as "typical". This can make it harder to read long passages of text. Printing on coloured paper and using dyslexia-friendly fonts can help those with dyslexia read more easily.

- Chewing muscle
- Bone
- The outer ear (pinna) funnels sound deeper into the ear.
- Fleshy earlobes dangle down.
- Fat
- Ear canal
- Bony cartilage provides structure.
- Outer ear

TAKE A SEAT

Sitting down for long periods can make you feel stiff. But your supportive skeleton allows you to shift positions and stay comfy – most of the time!

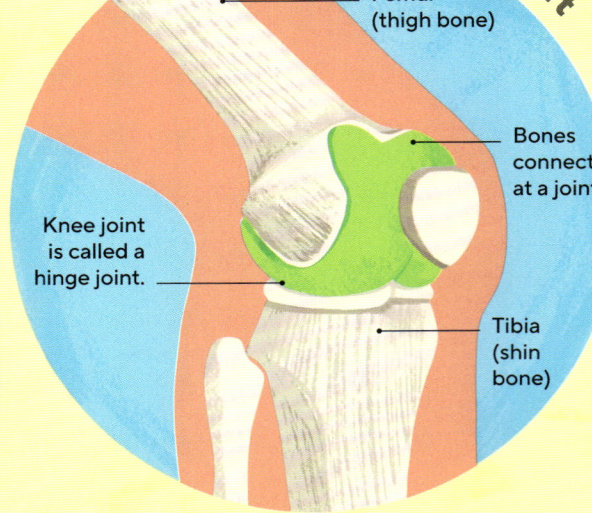

Knee joint
- Femur (thigh bone)
- Bones connect at a joint.
- Knee joint is called a hinge joint.
- Tibia (shin bone)

WHY CAN KNUCKLE CRACKING MAKE A NOISE?

When two or more bones meet, they form a joint. But they don't completely touch – they are separated by a fluid that prevents them from scraping against each other. If you pull your fingers or crack your knuckles, tiny gas bubbles inside the fluid burst – sometimes creating a sudden popping sound!

Finger joint is pulled on or cracked.

HOW DO YOU SIT CROSS-LEGGED?

The bones in your legs meet each other at moveable joints. In the same way a door on a hinge can swing back and forth, your knee joint allows you to move your lower leg up and down – bending or straightening the whole leg. Joints in your hip allow you to turn your legs inward.

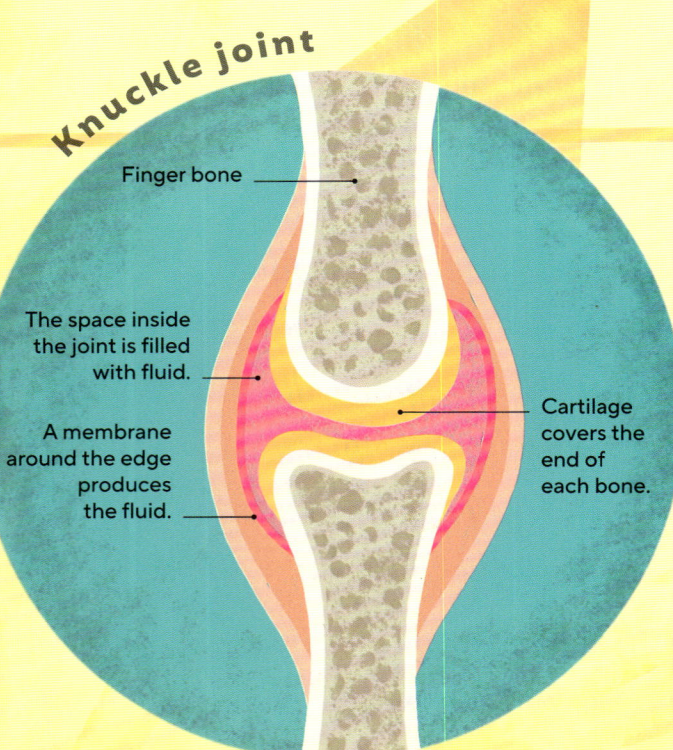

Knuckle joint
- Finger bone
- The space inside the joint is filled with fluid.
- A membrane around the edge produces the fluid.
- Cartilage covers the end of each bone.

58

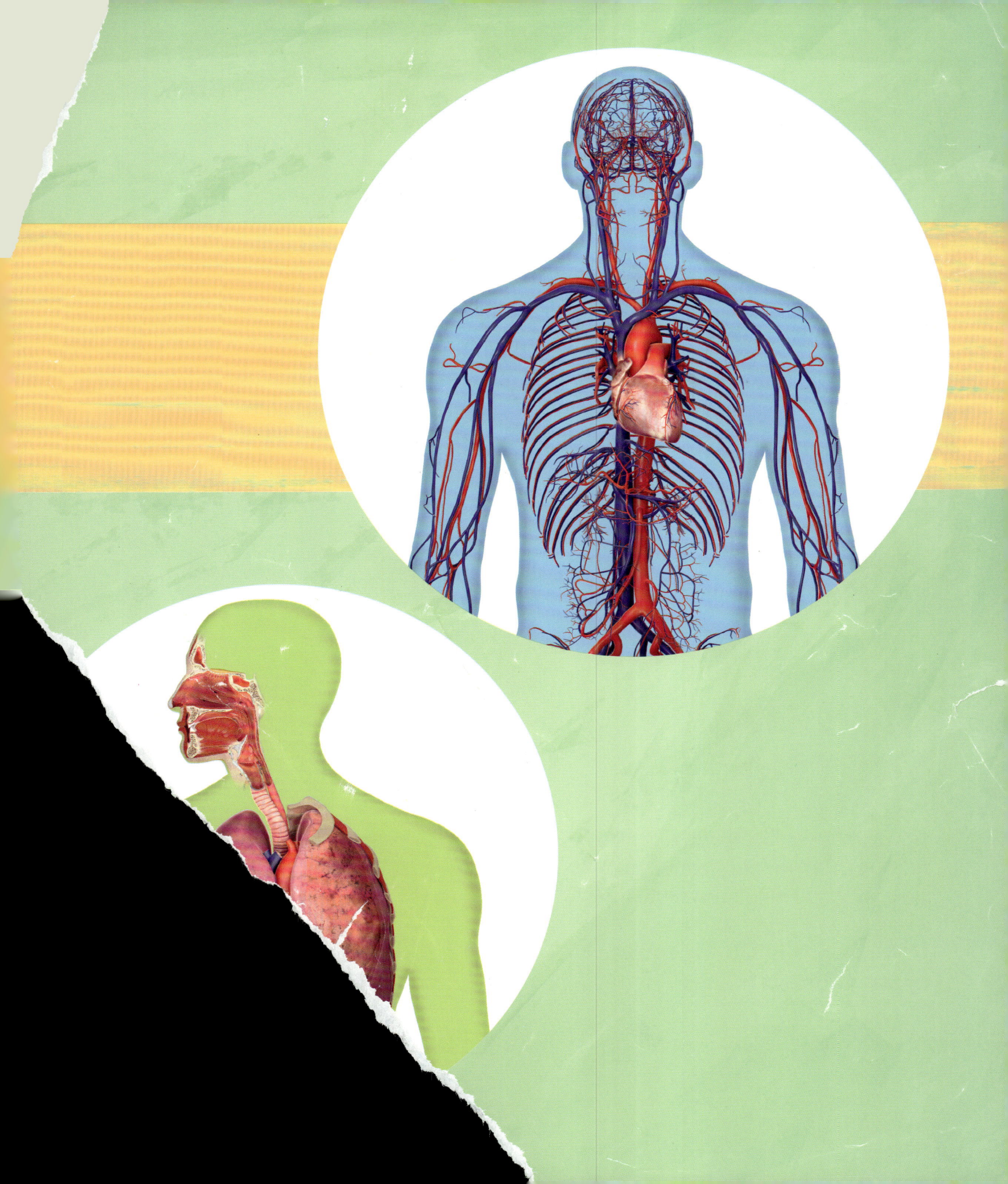

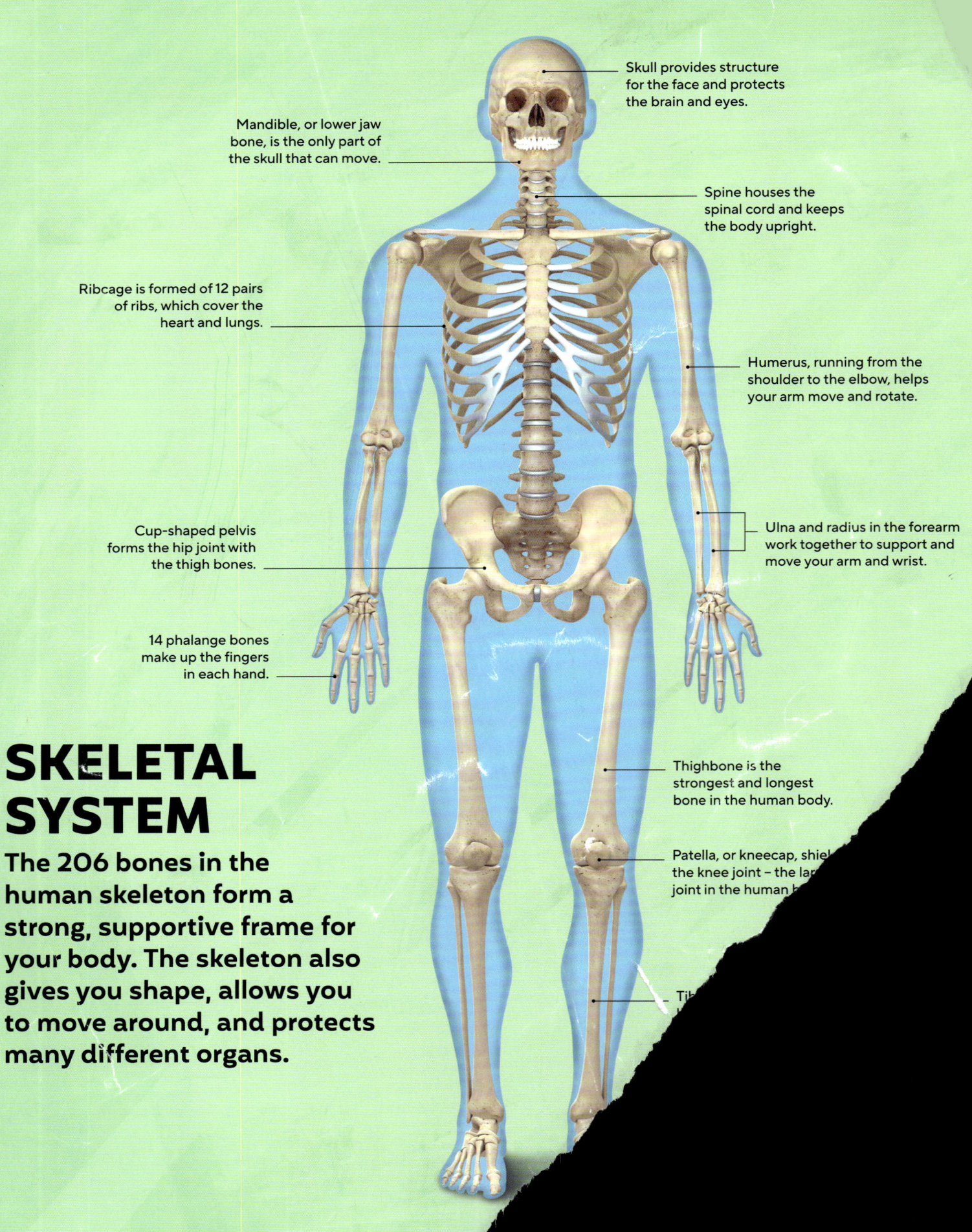

Skull provides structure for the face and protects the brain and eyes.

Mandible, or lower jaw bone, is the only part of the skull that can move.

Spine houses the spinal cord and keeps the body upright.

Ribcage is formed of 12 pairs of ribs, which cover the heart and lungs.

Humerus, running from the shoulder to the elbow, helps your arm move and rotate.

Cup-shaped pelvis forms the hip joint with the thigh bones.

Ulna and radius in the forearm work together to support and move your arm and wrist.

14 phalange bones make up the fingers in each hand.

Thighbone is the strongest and longest bone in the human body.

Patella, or kneecap, shie[lds] the knee joint – the la[rgest] joint in the human b[ody.]

Tib[ia]

SKELETAL SYSTEM

The 206 bones in the human skeleton form a strong, supportive frame for your body. The skeleton also gives you shape, allows you to move around, and protects many different organs.

WHAT SUPPORTS YOU WHEN YOU SIT DOWN?

Throughout the day your upper body stays balanced and supported by several bones fused together to make up your pelvis. This not only carries your weight when you sit down, but also protects organs such as your bladder and intestines and, in women, the uterus.

Sacrum (lower spine)

Large hip bones sit on each side.

Ischium (in yellow) and pubis (in green) are bones that form part of the pelvis.

Pelvis

Why do you fidget?

A lot of people move around and fidget when sitting still for long periods. Scientists aren't sure exactly why. It is thought that we fidget when we get distracted or struggle to pay attention, but fidgeting could also be a way of making us focus in these situations.

WHY DO YOU GET PINS AND NEEDLES?

If you put pressure on your legs or feet when sitting, blood vessels get squashed and your leg nerves don't get the oxygen-rich blood they need. Then, when you move, blood comes rushing back and the nerves wake up. But they overreact and send lots of confused signals to the brain, creating that strange tingling feeling.

Blood vessels supply blood to your legs and feet.

Lots of different nerves run all the way down to your heels and toes.

TRICKY TACKLE

Taking a shot in the school yard can sometimes end in more of a stumble than a success. Any scrapes and scratches must be speedily patched up by your body.

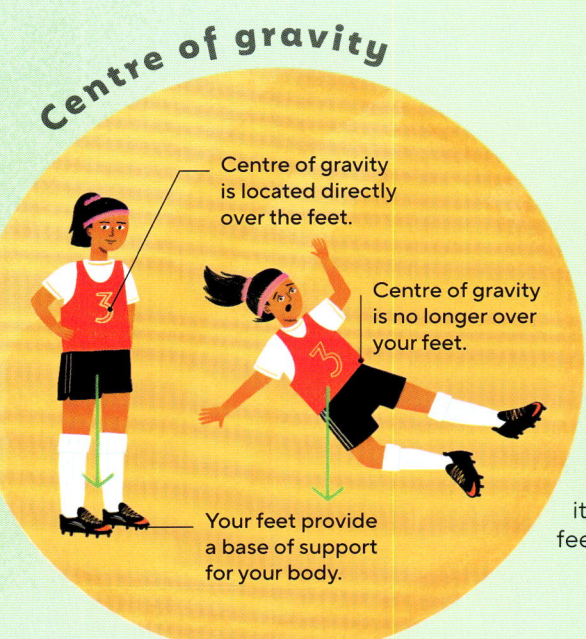

Centre of gravity

Centre of gravity is located directly over the feet.

Centre of gravity is no longer over your feet.

Your feet provide a base of support for your body.

Why do you have to clean wounds?

Your body is good at healing. But if dirt and bacteria get inside the wound, they can cause an infection, which makes the wound take longer to heal. Rinsing the cut area with clean water, and cleaning it with soap or antiseptic wipes, can prevent harmful substances from getting inside.

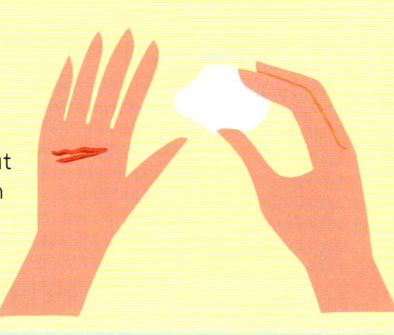

WHY DO YOU FALL OVER?

Your body has a centre of gravity – a point around which it is balanced – somewhere around your belly button. When you stand, your centre of gravity is supported by your feet below it. But leaning too far moves most of your body away from the feet, causing you to topple over!

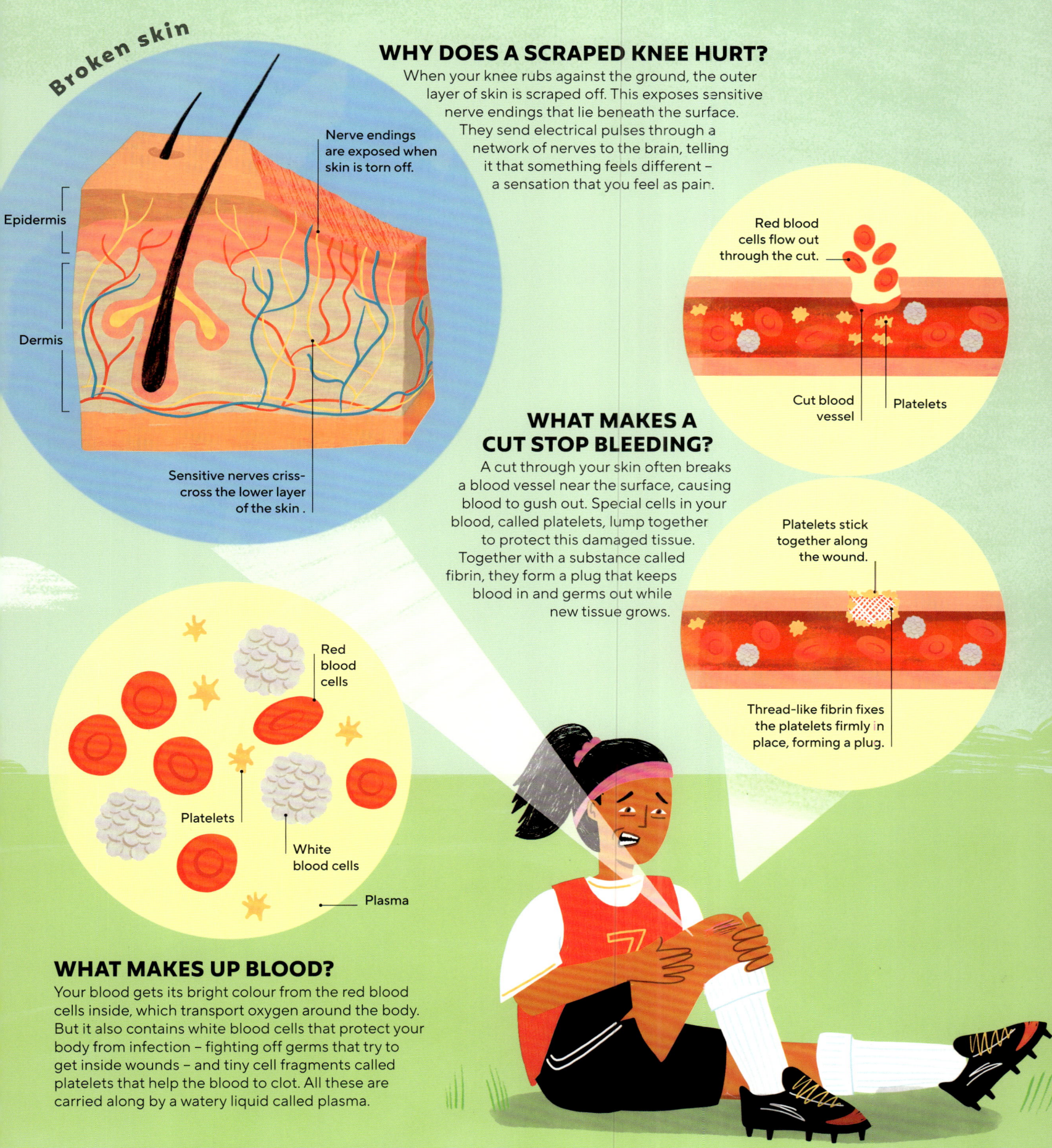

Broken skin

WHY DOES A SCRAPED KNEE HURT?

When your knee rubs against the ground, the outer layer of skin is scraped off. This exposes sensitive nerve endings that lie beneath the surface. They send electrical pulses through a network of nerves to the brain, telling it that something feels different – a sensation that you feel as pain.

Nerve endings are exposed when skin is torn off.

Epidermis

Dermis

Sensitive nerves criss-cross the lower layer of the skin.

Red blood cells flow out through the cut.

Cut blood vessel

Platelets

WHAT MAKES A CUT STOP BLEEDING?

A cut through your skin often breaks a blood vessel near the surface, causing blood to gush out. Special cells in your blood, called platelets, lump together to protect this damaged tissue. Together with a substance called fibrin, they form a plug that keeps blood in and germs out while new tissue grows.

Platelets stick together along the wound.

Thread-like fibrin fixes the platelets firmly in place, forming a plug.

Red blood cells

Platelets

White blood cells

Plasma

WHAT MAKES UP BLOOD?

Your blood gets its bright colour from the red blood cells inside, which transport oxygen around the body. But it also contains white blood cells that protect your body from infection – fighting off germs that try to get inside wounds – and tiny cell fragments called platelets that help the blood to clot. All these are carried along by a watery liquid called plasma.

ACCIDENTS HAPPEN

While some injuries can be very serious, others are a normal part of life. Some scratches and scrapes will heal naturally on their own but others may need medical attention.

SPLINTER
A sharp piece of wood, glass, metal, or other material that becomes embedded in the skin is called a splinter. Small splinters can be easily removed using tweezers, but deeper ones are more difficult to remove and may need a doctor's help.

BRUISE
Appearing in a wide range of unsettling colours – from red and purple to brown and yellow – bruises are marks on your body that are painful to touch. They form when you bump or fall on a part of your body. This causes blood vessels to break, leaking blood under the surface of your skin. Some people form bruises more easily than others.

Splinters break through the surface of the skin.

CRAMP

A sudden, sharp, and unexpected pain in your leg is known as a cramp. This happens when muscles in the leg tighten, making it hard to move. Cramps can happen for a number of reasons, from dehydration to overusing a muscle, but they usually go away in a short amount of time.

Muscle cramps are most common in the legs and the feet.

BROKEN BONE

When someone has fractured a bone, you will often see their limb in a plaster cast. This stops their broken bone from moving around, after a doctor has placed it in the correct position to naturally heal. Most people will wear casts for around 6–8 weeks while the bone fuses back together.

Casts around broken bones are commonly made of fibreglass – a lightweight plastic that can be easily cut off when the bone has healed.

FIRST-DEGREE BURN

A first-degree burn damages only the top and outer layer of the skin, called the epidermis. You might get this type of burn from spilling a hot drink or by accidentally touching hot cooking equipment. The burn usually looks red on pale skin and reddish-brown on darker skin, and may feel sore and later blister. You should seek medical attention for burns.

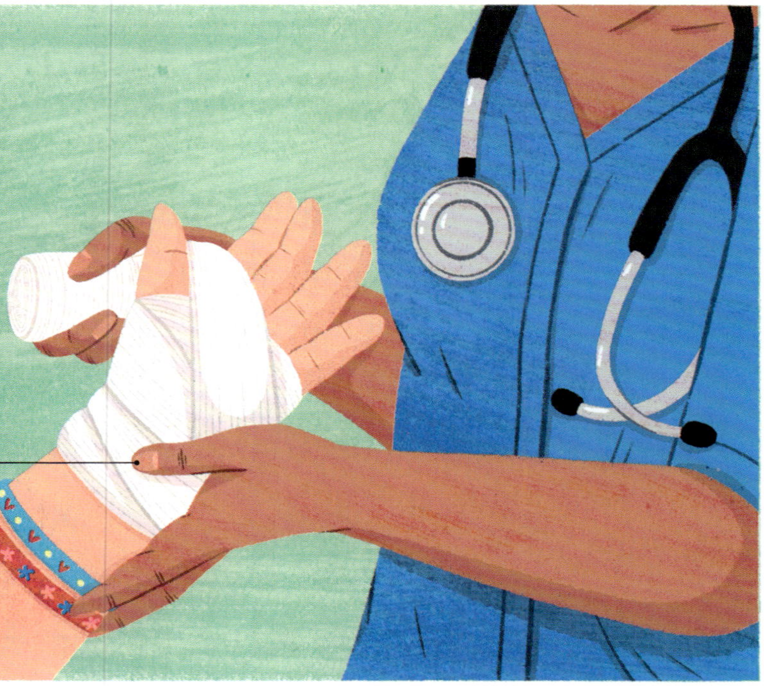

A loose dressing wrapped around the burn area will protect it from germs as it heals.

GRAB A BITE

Your mouth may water and your stomach rumble before you eat lunch. Be sure to chew each morsel well so it can travel down your throat to your stomach.

WHY CAN SPICY FOODS MAKE YOU FEEL LIKE YOUR MOUTH IS BURNING?

Spicy foods contain a substance called capsaicin. This triggers nerves in the mouth that normally detect heat, making your body think it is overheating. Your body attempts to clear out the cause of the problem by making you sweat, and get a runny nose, and your mouth may feel like it is burning!

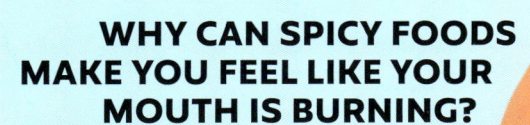

1. Intestine walls contract here.
2. This section relaxes.
3. Food moves along propelled by frequent waves of muscle contractions.

WHY DOES YOUR STOMACH RUMBLE?

All parts of your digestive tract – from oesophagus to anus – have muscular walls that contract to constantly push food along. This process is known as peristalsis and may cause growling noises! It is thought that you especially hear noises when you are hungry, as the stomach and intestines have less food inside them to muffle the sounds.

WHY DOESN'T FOOD GO DOWN THE WRONG WAY?

To make sure your food does not end up in the lungs instead of the stomach, your throat changes shape when you swallow. A flap of cartilage called the epiglottis folds downwards, blocking the entrance to your windpipe. Part of the roof of your mouth also blocks air from the nose from entering until the food passes through.

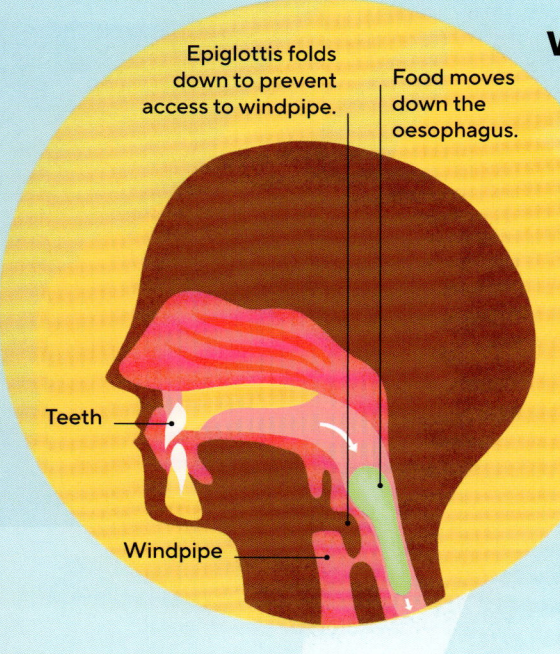

Epiglottis folds down to prevent access to windpipe.
Food moves down the oesophagus.
Teeth
Windpipe

HOW DO YOU CHEW FOOD?

Most of the bones in your head are hard and immoveable, forming the skull, which protects the brain. But your lower jawbone, known as the mandible, is the only bone in the face that can move. Strong muscles (see page 104) pull it up and down, allowing your upper and lower teeth to meet with a powerful bite, crushing food between them.

The mandible moves the mouth open and closed.

Why can some people tolerate more spice than others?

Both nature and nurture are thought to affect how you feel about spicy food. Scientists think some people might have genes that help them tolerate higher levels of spice, but your spice sensitivity is also affected by how frequently you eat those kinds of food. Repeatedly eating spicy snacks will probably increase the level of heat you like.

65

MAKING MUSIC

Practice makes perfect for lots of skills and making a melody is no different. Using both hands in different ways at the same time gives your brain a good workout.

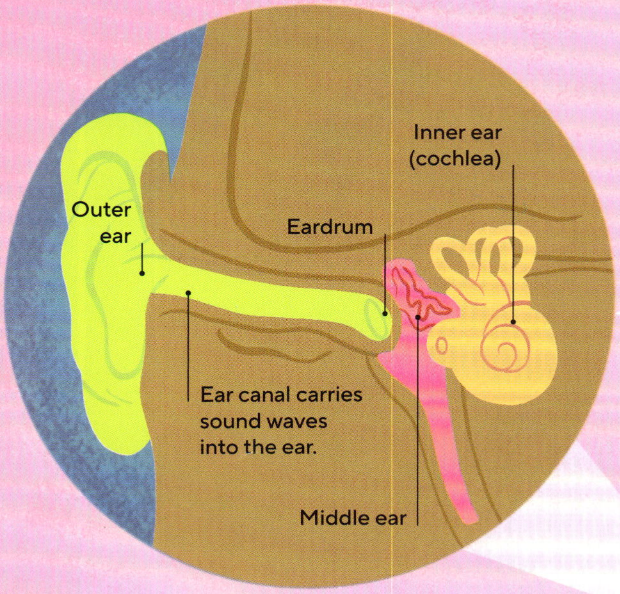

Outer ear · **Eardrum** · **Inner ear (cochlea)** · **Ear canal carries sound waves into the ear.** · **Middle ear**

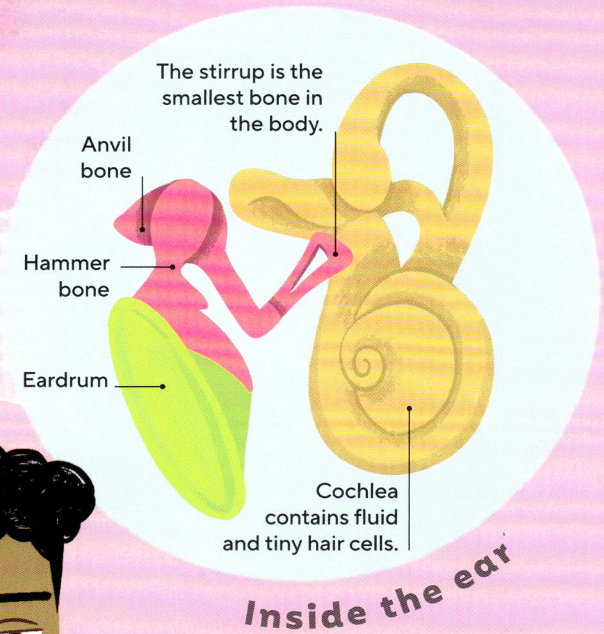

The stirrup is the smallest bone in the body. · **Anvil bone** · **Hammer bone** · **Eardrum** · **Cochlea contains fluid and tiny hair cells.**

Inside the ear

WHERE DO SOUNDS THAT REACH YOUR EAR GO?

The ear is made up of three main parts. Sounds are funnelled in by the fleshy outer ear, until they hit the eardrum – a thin film at the entrance to the middle ear. They cause it to vibrate, a movement that is picked up by three tiny bones and passed on to the inner ear. A fluid-filled part called the cochlea then converts the vibrations into signals that are sent to the brain to be processed.

Is playing music good for the brain?

Regularly practising music is a great way of keeping the brain healthy. It uses many parts of the brain and body and requires input from multiple senses. Playing a piano or keyboard is thought to be especially beneficial, perhaps because the brain has to coordinate the actions of different fingers.

Brain hemispheres

The corpus callosum connects both hemispheres.

The left brain is thought to deal with logic.

The cerebellum helps coordinate muscle movements.

The right brain deals with creativity.

Tendons

Tendons attach to forearm muscles.

These muscles help you to spread out your fingers.

Tendons pull on the finger bones to help them bend.

HOW DO YOUR FINGERS BEND AND MOVE?

Your fingers don't actually contain any muscles! Instead long strips of tissue called tendons run down through your hand to your fingertips. They work like the strings of a puppet, pulling and releasing the fingers. Small muscles in the palm also help you to grip.

HOW CAN YOUR HANDS DO DIFFERENT THINGS AT THE SAME TIME?

Playing an instrument uses many different areas of the brain – some areas control parts of the body and others have special functions. These areas are split across two hemispheres (see page 101). A bridge of nerves called the corpus callosum connects both sides and enables them to work together.

What is envy?

Envy is about wanting something that someone else has – whether it's a skill, a possession, or even a trait such as confidence. It often happens when you compare yourself to others, or feel insecure about your own abilities. It can also happen when you feel a situation is unfair or a person does not deserve what they have.

Is it normal to feel envious?

Envy is a common human emotion that everyone experiences at some point. It can even be helpful at times. When we see things in others that we want for ourselves, it can help us to identify our own goals and motivate us towards achieving them.

What happens when you feel envious?

Feeling envious might make you feel unhappy and insecure, or angry and frustrated. You may be more likely to act unfairly or harshly towards those around you, but it is important to remember that taking your feelings out on others will not make you feel less envious.

Can you be competitive without envy?

Yes! It is possible to have a healthy competition where you feel confident in your own abilities and are supportive of your opponents. For example, if you finish second place in a race, you can congratulate the person who won and acknowledge that you tried your best.

What should I do when I feel envious?

- Try to understand why you're feeling this way and what has bothered you.

- Add "but luckily..." to your envious thought – "I lost this time but luckily I can try again next year!"

- Focus on your own achievements. You may not have run faster than another person but you might have beat your own personal best!

FEELING ENVIOUS

Finishing second place can be tough, especially when you've given it your all. Although it is normal to feel envious of other people, it can be helpful to use this emotion to motivate yourself.

Are envy and jealousy the same thing?

Although the two feelings are linked, they have different meanings. Envy is about wanting what someone else has, whereas jealousy is a fear of someone taking what you already have. For example, a person might feel jealous if a parent is giving time and attention to a new sibling.

ZOOMING OUT

DNA is a structure so small it can only be seen under a microscope. But where in the body is it found?

From cells...
Cells inside your body carry DNA within them – packed tightly into their round centres (known as the nucleus).

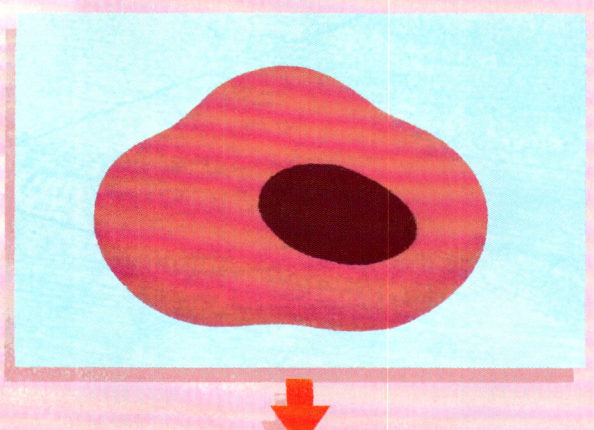

...to tissues...
Clusters of lots of tiny individual cells that all have similar functions group together to form a tissue.

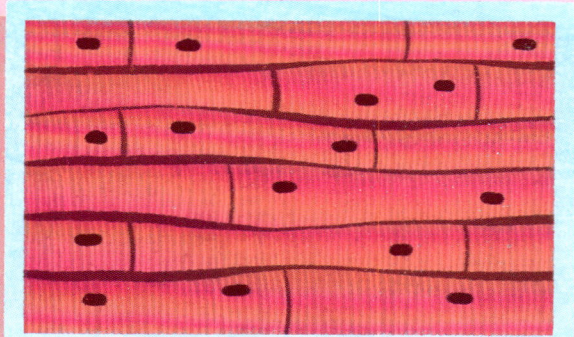

...to muscles
The tough muscles that pull on your skeleton are all made of bundles of fibres of muscle tissue.

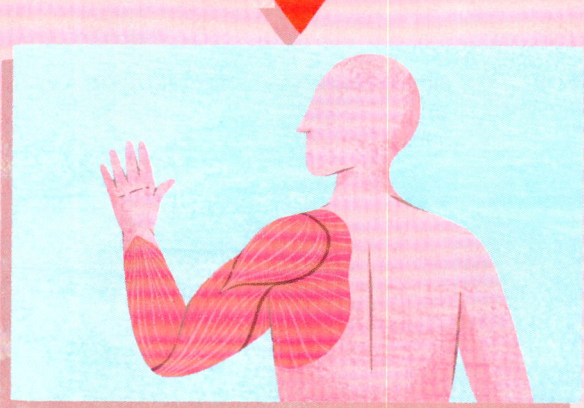

IF YOU STRETCHED OUT THE DNA IN ONE CELL IT WOULD BE 2 M (6.6 FT) LONG!

The DNA strand continually twists around on itself to form a spiral shape.

Two long strips form the outer backbone of the DNA ladder.

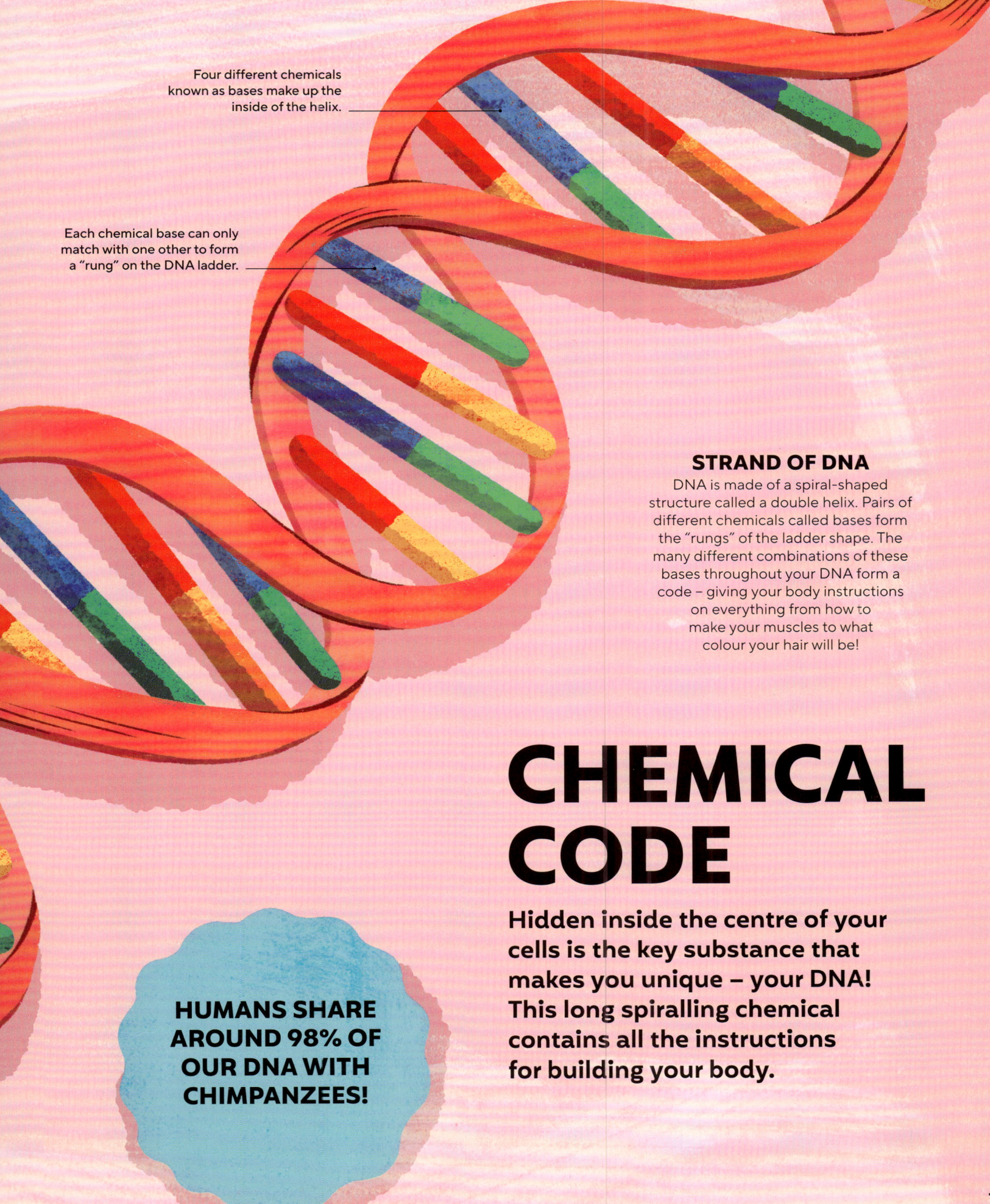

Four different chemicals known as bases make up the inside of the helix.

Each chemical base can only match with one other to form a "rung" on the DNA ladder.

STRAND OF DNA

DNA is made of a spiral-shaped structure called a double helix. Pairs of different chemicals called bases form the "rungs" of the ladder shape. The many different combinations of these bases throughout your DNA form a code – giving your body instructions on everything from how to make your muscles to what colour your hair will be!

CHEMICAL CODE

Hidden inside the centre of your cells is the key substance that makes you unique – your DNA! This long spiralling chemical contains all the instructions for building your body.

HUMANS SHARE AROUND 98% OF OUR DNA WITH CHIMPANZEES!

MAKE A SPLASH

Every powerful plunge you make beneath the water moves your body forward. Blood is pumped to your limbs to allow your muscles to carry out every stroke and kick.

Inside an artery

- A layer of tough, thick muscle
- Blood is pumped through the artery at high pressure.
- Expandable elastic layer

Arteries in the leg

- A network of arteries spreads through the legs.
- The posterior tibial artery supplies blood to the calf and foot muscles.

HOW DO ARTERIES WORK?

Arteries have much thicker walls than veins (see page 43). This is because the blood that travels through them is pumped from the heart at high pressure. As well as containing a layer of tough muscle to help withstand this pressure, a stretchy elastic layer below allows them to temporarily stretch and bounce back.

WHAT POWERS YOUR MUSCLES?

As you exercise, your muscles need to be constantly supplied with energy. Blood vessels called arteries carry blood containing oxygen and nutrients from the heart to all the muscles across your body. They use the oxygen and nutrients to generate energy.

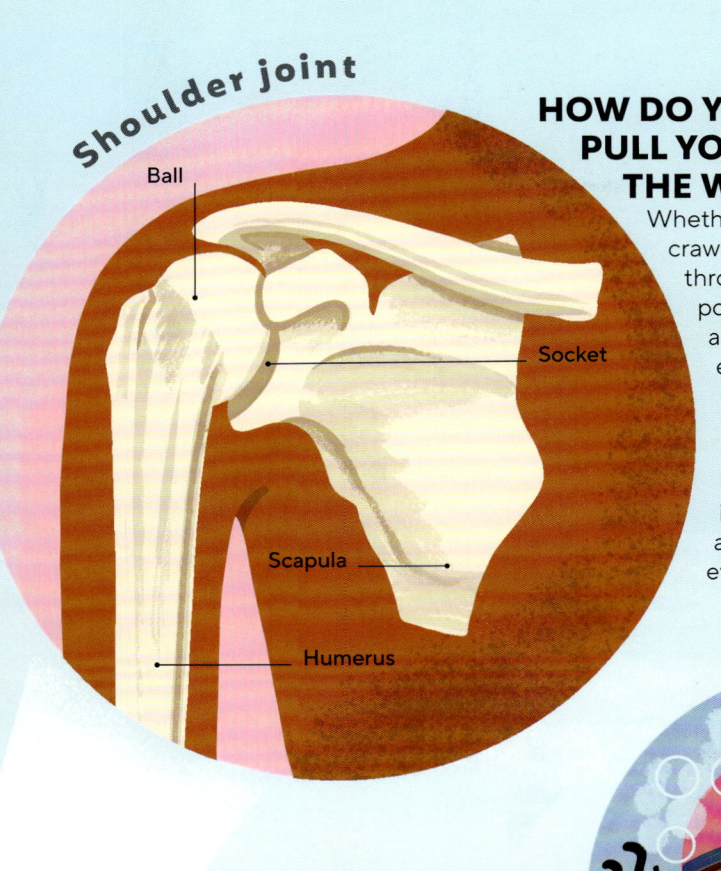

HOW DO YOUR ARMS PULL YOU THROUGH THE WATER?

Whether you are doing front crawl or breaststroke, striking through the water involves a powerful action from your arm. It is able to swing around easily because your shoulder is a type of joint called a ball and socket joint. Here, one bone (such as the humerus) fits into a cup-like dent in the other bone and is able to rotate in almost every direction.

Why do you float?

If you bob upright when you are in water, you will sink. But if you lie flat on your back, you should be able to float. This is because you are spread across the water and have a larger surface area than when standing. Lots of air inside our lungs makes us lighter than the water, so as long as you do not swallow too much water, you should not start to sink!

HOW LONG CAN YOU HOLD YOUR BREATH UNDER WATER?

On average, people can hold their breath for between 30 and 90 seconds, but your body makes this hard! Special nerve cells notice when carbon dioxide builds up in the blood and the cells in the lungs notice when they stop inflating. These trigger the brain to increase the urge to breathe, encouraging you to return to your normal breathing rate (see pages 22–23).

BEING UNDERWATER TRIGGERS A NATURAL RESPONSE IN THE BODY TO **CONSERVE OXYGEN AND PROTECT THE ORGANS** AT DEPTH.

THE BODY'S IMMEDIATE REACTION TO BEING IN WATER IS TO **SLOW THE HEART RATE** BY UP TO 30% TO SAVE OXYGEN.

BLOOD VESSELS IN THE LIMBS CONSTRICT, SENDING OXYGEN-RICH BLOOD TO THE **MAJOR ORGANS,** WHERE IT IS MOST NEEDED.

AS A DIVER GOES DEEPER, THE **CHEST CAVITY FILLS WITH BLOOD** TO PREVENT THE LUNGS BEING CRUSHED BY WATER PRESSURE.

PRESSURE AND COLD BOTH AFFECT THE **HORMONE THAT CONTROLS URINATION,** RESULTING IN A DIVER'S URGENT NEED TO PEE!

FREE DIVERS, WHO DIVE WITH NO AIR SUPPLY, TRAIN TO **REDUCE THEIR HEART RATE TO 50%** OF ITS NORMAL RATE.

THE RECORD FOR THE **LONGEST TIME SPENT UNDERWATER** WITHOUT BREATHING APPARATUS IS 24 MINUTES 37.36 SECONDS!

THE BODY UNDERWATER

COLD WATER CAN SHOCK THE BODY, TRIGGERING A **VERY RAPID HEARTBEAT**.

Humans are adapted to live on dry land, so being deep underwater puts the body under immense strain. We cannot breathe in water, so have to carry our own air supply for all but the shortest dives. Water pressure is a key issue – the deeper you dive, the greater the volume of water pressing on your vital organs. And if the water is cold, diving becomes even more dangerous!

WATER CREATES MORE RESISTANCE THAN AIR SO THE **MUSCLES WORK UP TO 15% HARDER** UNDERWATER.

DIVERS MUST HEAD BACK UP TO THE SURFACE **SLOWLY** TO AVOID HARMFUL **BUBBLES FORMING IN THEIR BLOOD**.

TIME FOR A BREAK

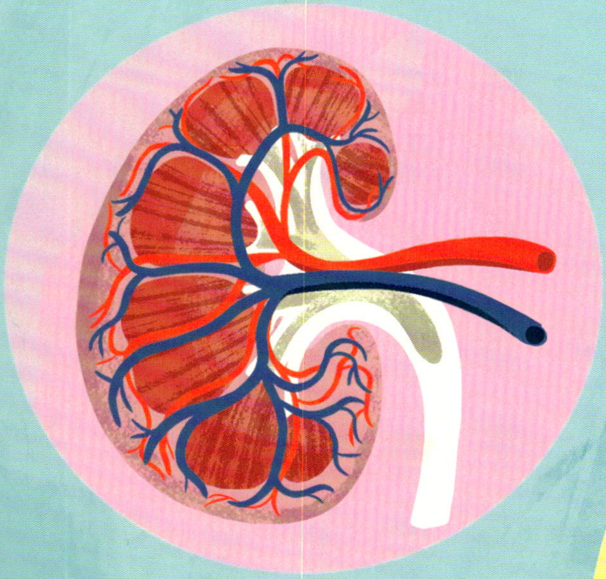

GOT TO GO

Regular toilet trips are a part of everyday life. As you dash to the bathroom to relieve that urge, your bladder is readying itself to get rid of excess water and waste.

Kidney nephron

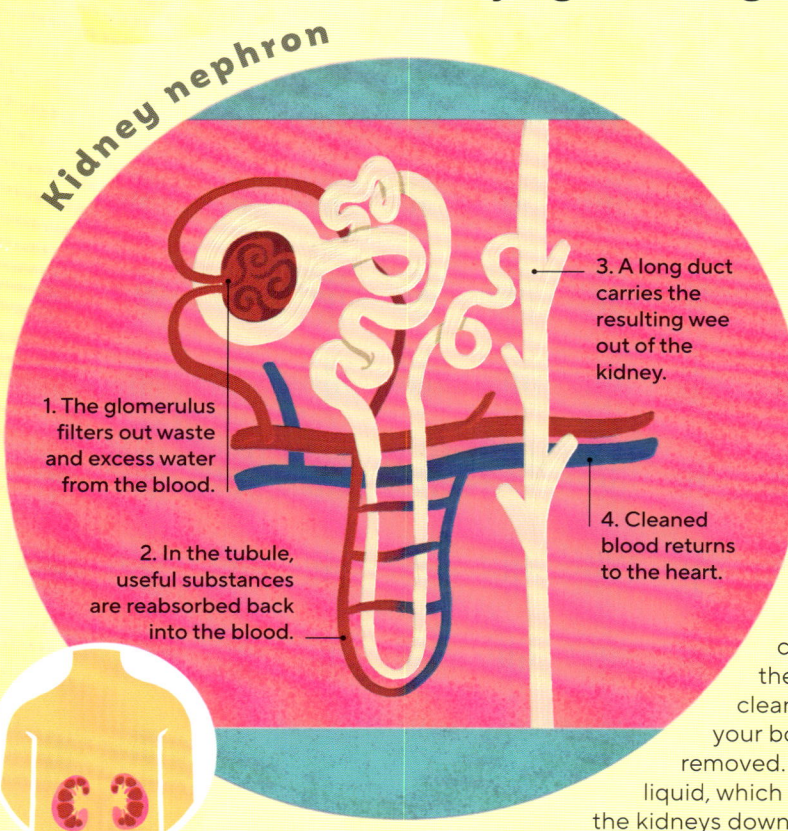

1. The glomerulus filters out waste and excess water from the blood.
2. In the tubule, useful substances are reabsorbed back into the blood.
3. A long duct carries the resulting wee out of the kidney.
4. Cleaned blood returns to the heart.

Why do you have two kidneys?

Lots of organs in your body come in pairs. Scientists think this could be so that we have a back-up in case one fails. A healthy person can even donate one of their kidneys to someone who needs one. The remaining kidney has to work a bit harder, but regular tests can check that it is doing its job fine.

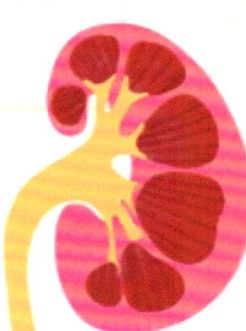

WHERE IS WEE MADE?

Wee, or urine, is produced in the kidneys. Each kidney has millions of tiny filters, called nephrons. As blood passes through these squiggly structures, it is cleaned and any waste or water your body doesn't need is removed. This forms a yellow liquid, which passes from the kidneys down to your bladder.

DOES CROSSING YOUR LEGS HELP YOU HOLD WEE IN?

In desperate situations, crossing your legs – mainly while standing – can help squeeze shut the urethra (a tube that carries wee out of the body). However, it is best not to hold your wee in for too long and to get to a toilet as soon as possible.

Female pelvis

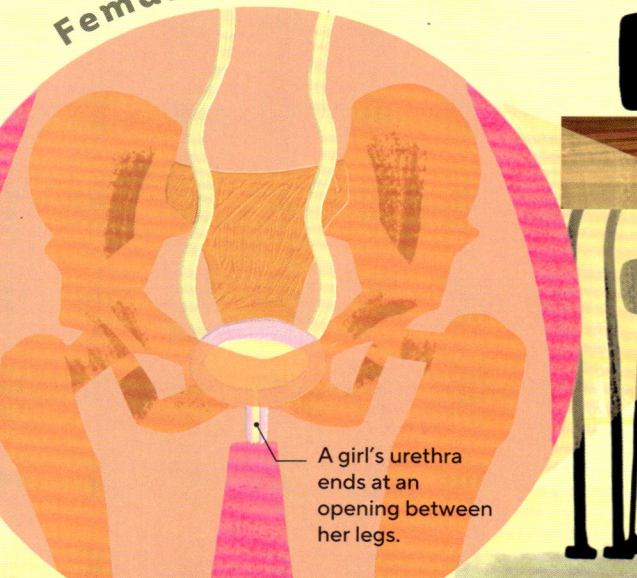

A girl's urethra ends at an opening between her legs.

HOW DO YOU KNOW WHEN YOU NEED TO WEE?

Urine enters your bladder from the kidneys, pushing on the bladder wall and causing it to expand like a balloon as it fills up. Sensors in the stretched bladder wall then send a signal to the brain – letting you know it is time to go. When you are ready to wee, muscle rings at the bottom of the bladder relax, releasing wee out of the body, through a tube called the urethra.

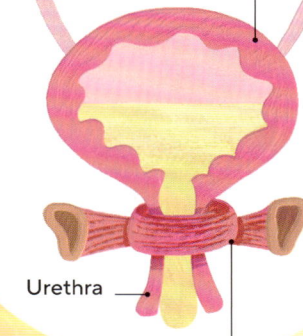

Tubes called ureters carry wee from the kidneys to the bladder.

The bladder expands as wee pushes against it.

Wall muscles contract so the wee is pushed out.

Urethra

Muscle rings contract and relax, regulating the flow of wee.

Why is wee sometimes a different colour?

Urine colour depends mostly on how hydrated your body is. That is why it can be darker in the morning, when you have not had anything to drink for several hours. Certain foods can also change the colour. For example, beetroot can turn wee a surprising shade of red, and asparagus can make it green.

Wee that has a very pale colour means you are drinking enough water.

This might be the colour of a morning wee, if you haven't had anything to drink since the evening.

Dark yellow wee shows you are dehydrated, and need to drink more water.

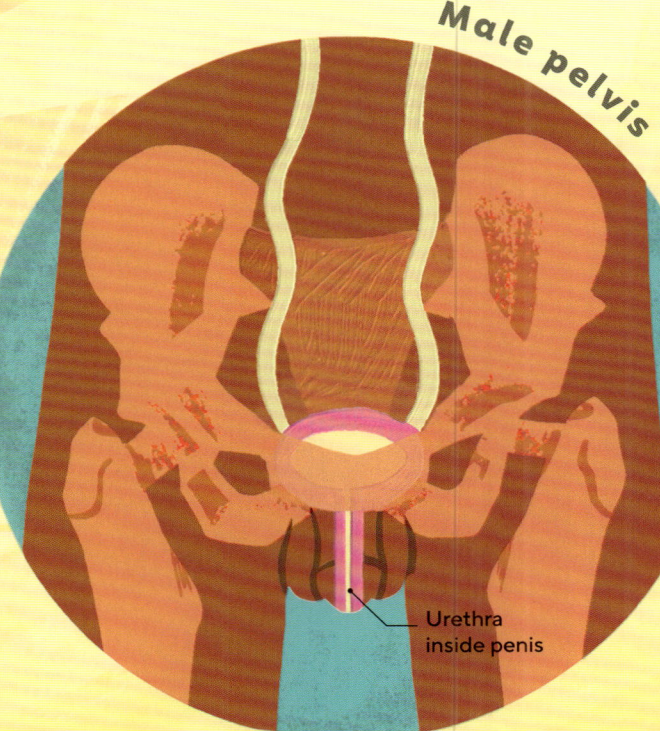

Male pelvis

Urethra inside penis

WHY CAN BOYS WEE STANDING UP?

The urethra that carries urine from the bladder and out of the body is longer in boys. Instead of travelling a short distance to end at an opening between the legs (as in girls), it passes down the length of a boy's penis. The opening being further away makes it easier for boys to aim their wee away from themselves while standing.

AT THE MUSEUM

A field trip might be a feast for your eyes and brain, but your legs will soon get tired from all that wandering around. A short sit-down gives your body time to rest and recover.

Why don't you have a tail?

Humans and modern monkeys evolved from the same common ancestor, a creature that used their tail for balance when climbing through the treetops. Although we lost the tail around 25 million years ago, we still have a bone in the pelvis (see pages 58–59) which would have previously supported a tail. Today, babies growing in the uterus initially develop a tiny tail, but this disappears before they are born.

WHERE IS YOUR LARGEST MUSCLE?

There are several muscles in your bum, but the main one – the gluteus maximus – is actually the largest muscle in your body. Together, these muscles not only help you sit down comfortably, but also ensure that when you rise from a seated position and walk upright, your pelvis is in a stable position.

Bum muscles

The gluteus medius helps move the hip joint.

Gluteus maximus

Default brain

Certain parts of the brain are more active when you are not engaged in a specific task.

The default mode network is spread across different brain areas.

Is sitting down too much bad for you?

Your body needs to keep regularly moving. Scientists know that spending too much time sitting down throughout the day can increase your risk of various health problems. If you have to sit for long periods, taking a quick stretch or stroll to break this up can help.

WHAT DOES YOUR BRAIN DO WHEN YOU ARE RESTING AND SITTING DOWN?

Scientists using scanners to study brain activity have observed that certain parts "light up" when you take part in specific tasks. This shows the pathways between the nerve cells (see pages 110–111) are being used and that area is active. But new research has shown that some parts of the brain activate when you are not doing anything at all. Researchers call these areas the "default mode network" and think they could be responsible for creating daydreams, remembering events, and preparing for future social situations.

English braille

Braille dots are raised so you can feel them with your fingers.

HOW CAN YOU READ WITH YOUR FINGERS?

Blind or partially sighted children often use braille to read, as this language can be read with fingers rather than eyes. Braille works like a code, using combinations of six raised dots to represent the letters of the alphabet and numbers. Braille can be applied to many languages and this caption is written in English braille. The picture might give you a clue to what it says!

CATCHING UP

Break time can be a clamour of busy voices, as you chatter with friends. But you don't just communicate with words – your face, hands, and body language also play a part.

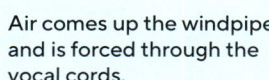

WHERE DOES YOUR VOICE COME FROM?

The sounds you make are produced by bands of tissue in your throat called vocal cords, which make up an area known as the voice box. When you are not speaking and are breathing normally, these cords sit in an open position. But when you talk, they close up and the air squeezing through them causes them to vibrate – producing sounds. Your mouth, lips, and tongue then shape these into words.

Voice box (larynx) sits in your windpipe.

Air comes up the windpipe and is forced through the vocal cords.

Closed vocal cords vibrate to make sounds.

Open vocal cords allow air in while breathing.

HOW DO YOU WHISPER?

The vocal folds are not closed when you whisper but instead are held apart a short way and stretched so tightly that they cannot vibrate. Air passes through them in a rush, which we hear as a high-pitched hiss.

Facial muscles stretch across the skull and neck.

Small *corrugator supercilii* muscles move your eyebrows into a frown.

Two muscles pull up the corners of your mouth into a smile.

Orbicularis oris muscles surround the mouth and help you pucker the lips when whistling (or kissing).

Why do boys get deeper voices as they get older?
During puberty, chemical messengers called hormones are produced. In boys, these cause their vocal cords to grow thicker and longer – making them generate deeper sounds. The cartilage around the voice box grows thicker in boys so that it sticks out from the throat in a little bump.

HOW DOES YOUR FACE CHANGE EXPRESSION?
There are more than 40 different muscles in the face (shown in many different colours or this illustration). They help us to chew, blink, and talk, but we also use them to show our emotions – whether we are happy, sad, surprised, or annoyed. Frowning moves the muscles above the nose and eyebrows, whereas when you smile those in your cheeks move.

WHAT IS SIGN LANGUAGE?
As well as using facial expressions, body language, and lip reading, sign language is a common method of communication used by those who are deaf or hard of hearing. There are more than 300 different sign languages worldwide, in which your hands and fingers are used to form words or letters.

Sign language
Crossing your two index fingers over each other and then swapping them forms the sign for "friend" in American Sign Language (ASL).

FLOWER POWER

A walk through the park brings many sights and scents. While some floral fragrances will delight, other plant particles may tickle your nose and cause you to sneeze!

Sense of smell

4. The olfactory bulb processes the smell.

3. Olfactory nerves carry signals to the olfactory bulb.

2. Smell receptors pick up the smells.

1. Smells travel through the nasal cavity as you breathe in.

HOW DO YOU SMELL?

When you inhale, tiny scent particles in the air are carried to the top of the nasal cavity. Here they are detected by smell receptors and processed by the olfactory bulb, a part of your brain that analyses smells. This is very closely connected to the parts of the brain that deal with memory and emotions, which is why certain smells can often remind you of a particular time or moment.

Does your nose grow as you age?

No, but it may look bigger! This is because the lower part of the nose is made of flexible cartilage, rather than hard bone. In elderly people, cartilage becomes less strong and elastic, and the skin looser, which can make the tip of the nose droop and appear larger.

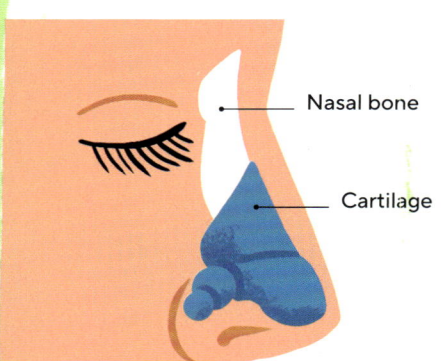

Nasal bone

Cartilage

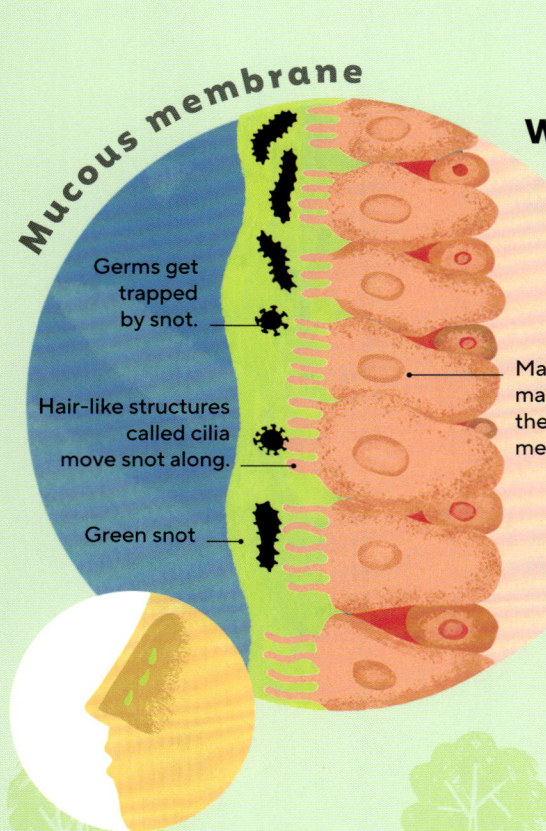

Mucous membrane
- Germs get trapped by snot.
- Hair-like structures called cilia move snot along.
- Green snot
- Many cells make up the mucous membrane.

WHY DO YOU MAKE SNOT?

This slimy substance keeps your nose moist but also has a defensive purpose, helping to wash away dust and germs. Soft tissues inside your nose, known as mucous membranes, produce snot. This is then pushed outwards by tiny hair-like structures. When you are unwell, you may produce more snot, to trap and remove the extra viruses and bacteria causing your sickness.

WHY DO YOU SNEEZE?

This explosive reflex kicks in when pollen, dust, or germs enter your nose and trigger the hairs inside. These send a signal to the brain, which responds by trying to clear out these irritants. As you sneeze, your eyes close automatically – possibly to stop the infected droplets that shoot out of your mouth and nose from entering your eyes.

Melanin in the skin
- Darker skin has more melanin distributed more evenly across its surface.
- Structures in the cell called melanosomes transport melanin to the surface.
- Melanocyte, a cell that produces melanin

WHAT MAKES SKIN GO DARKER IN THE SUN?

Inside your skin are special pigment-producing cells called melanocytes. Your skin colour is determined by both the types of pigment (melanin) that melanocytes produce and how this is distributed across the skin. All skin colours turn darker when exposed to sunlight, as your body produces extra melanin to protect against harmful rays. However, the protection it provides is only small, meaning no matter how dark your skin is, you still need to wear sunscreen!

ALLERGIES

Whether it's food or flowers, your busy immune system can sometimes interpret something harmless as a threat. In response, it panics your body into displaying a wide range of symptoms.

POLLEN AND DUST

Pollen grains – tiny particles produced by plants – can make many people sneeze when they are out and about at certain times of the year. But you might also find your nose tickling indoors, due to dust. This is actually an allergic reaction to the droppings of harmless microscopic creatures called dust mites.

ANIMALS

Being around fluffy animals such as dogs and cats can make some people sneeze; cough; and get itchy, watery eyes. You might think this is caused by hair or fur, but it is actually triggered by chemicals found in the animal's skin cells and saliva, which a pet can leave traces of around the house.

Cats shed dead skin cells, called dander, which can trigger allergies.

FOOD
Seemingly tasty foods such as nuts, milk, and shellfish are common foods that trigger allergic reactions in some people. They can cause itches, a rash, or swelling of the lips and face, as well as more severe symptoms. Recent research suggests children today are more likely to develop food allergies than in previous generations, but scientists don't know why this is!

Celery can cause swelling and itching around the mouth and lips.

INSECT STINGS
If a wasp or other insect stings you, an itchy lump may form. But some people have a much stronger allergic reaction – going into a state called anaphylaxis, where they can struggle to breathe and need urgent medical attention.

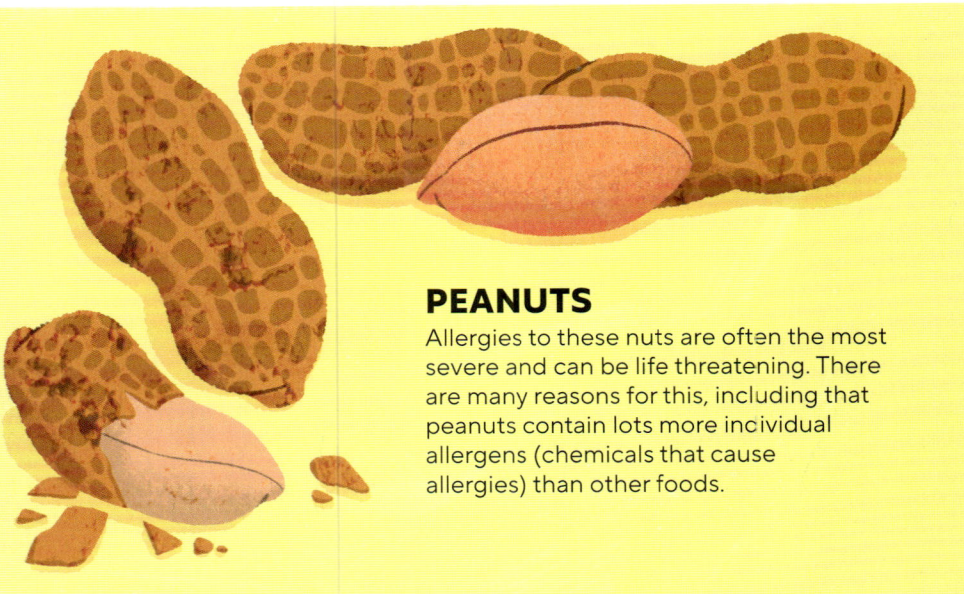

PEANUTS
Allergies to these nuts are often the most severe and can be life threatening. There are many reasons for this, including that peanuts contain lots more incividual allergens (chemicals that cause allergies) than other foods.

SCARY MOVIE

Beware! Ghosts and monsters may not be real, but seeing them jump out in a scary movie can make your body react as if they were. Being afraid is not just all in your head.

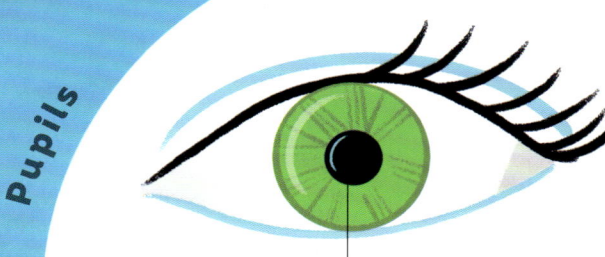

Pupils

Constricted pupil

Dilated pupil

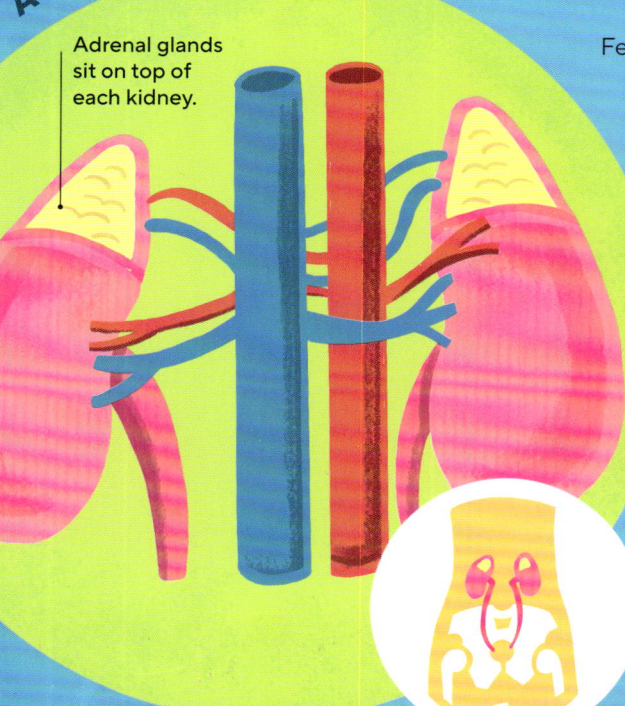

Adrenal glands

Adrenal glands sit on top of each kidney.

WHAT HAPPENS IN YOUR BRAIN?

Feeling fear starts in the brain, in a tiny almond-shaped region called the amygdala. This is part of the limbic system, which regulates emotions. The amygdala alerts your nervous system and triggers all the other body responses.

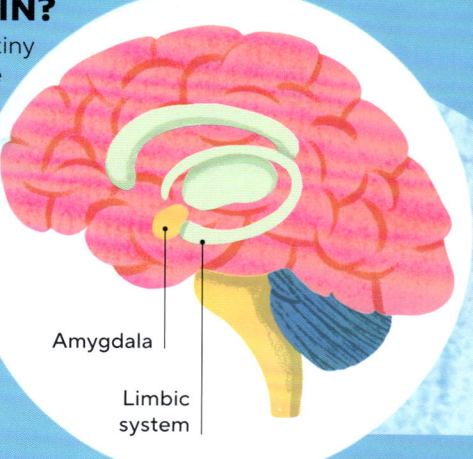

Amygdala

Limbic system

WHAT MAKES YOUR BODY RESPOND TO FEAR?

Located on the top of your kidneys are the adrenal glands. When you feel scared, these release a hormone called adrenaline into your bloodstream. This can happen very quickly – leading to an adrenaline rush. This sends your body into a "fight or flight mode", where it is ready to react quickly to stressful situations.

WHY DO YOUR PUPILS CHANGE SIZE?

Normally, it is the level of light that affects how big your pupils are. They dilate (get bigger) in darker places to let in more light, and constrict (get smaller) when it is bright. But being afraid can also cause the pupils to dilate, so that your body has the best vision with which to face any threats.

Why does your heart race when you are scared?

The release of adrenaline causes your heart to beat faster. This allows it to provide more of the important sugars and oxygen needed for generating energy to key muscles and organs.

On a heart rate monitor, spikes shows when the heart beats.

The distance between spikes gets closer together when your heart beats faster.

WHY DO YOUR HANDS GET CLAMMY?

Sweat is produced to cool the body, but it is also triggered as part of the "fight or flight" response. This happens even though your hands might be cold, as blood is directed away from them towards major organs.

Inside the lungs

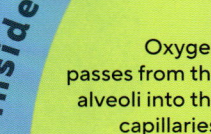

Oxygen passes from the alveoli into the capillaries.

Lots of tiny tubes in the lungs called bronchioles each end in alveoli.

A network of capillaries stretches over each alveolus.

WHAT MAKES YOU SHORT OF BREATH?

Breathing faster allows you to get more oxygen into your body. This travels through the many tubes of your lungs until it reaches tiny sacs called alveoli. From there it passes into blood vessels called capillaries (see page 22).

What makes you feel sad?

Lots of things in your daily life can cause sadness – from big events such as arguments with friends to something as small as breaking a favourite possession. Like all other emotions, sadness gives you information about yourself, and tells you when something is not right for you.

What happens when you are sad?

Feeling sad or low in mood can cause changes in how you behave. You may find you have less energy and that you do not feel like joining in or talking as much when you are with other people.

How can you help yourself feel better when you are sad?

- Identify someone you can talk to about your feelings. If you find it tricky to start this conversation, try writing a note to them instead.

- Spend time noticing what makes your mood change, so you can seek out more positive experiences.

- Try spending time outdoors and in nature to help boost your mood.

Why can sadness make you cry?
Crying can be a good way of releasing pent-up emotions and sharing your feelings with others. The tears you produce from feeling strong emotions are chemically different to those triggered by irritation, but scientists don't know why!

Is it normal to feel sad all the time?
Everyone experiences periods of sadness. But if you find yourself regularly having sad feelings that do not go away, it is best to speak to friends, family, a trusted adult, or a doctor about this.

Why can loneliness make you feel sad?
Spending time with other people you like makes your body produce feel-good chemicals. When you are feeling lonely and not as connected to people, you are more likely to feel sad.

FEELING SAD

The disappointment of a rainy day or missing plans with friends might make you feel a bit down. We all feel a little low sometimes, but there are many ways you can try to cheer yourself up.

CELEBRATE!

Having a birthday is not just a good reason for a party. It marks another year of your body growing and changing, and is an opportunity to eat delicious cake!

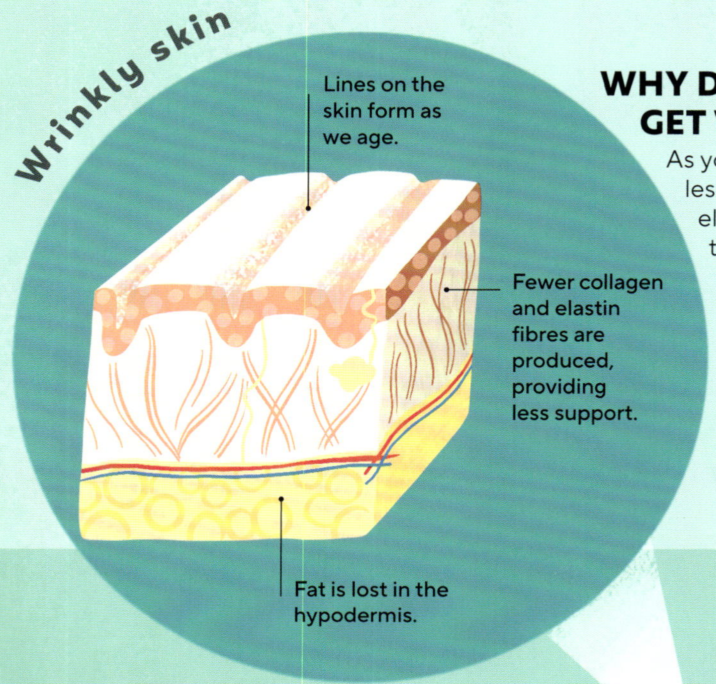

Wrinkly skin

- Lines on the skin form as we age.
- Fewer collagen and elastin fibres are produced, providing less support.
- Fat is lost in the hypodermis.

WHY DO PEOPLE GET WRINKLES?

As you age, your skin will begin to produce less substances called collagen and elastin, which help keep the skin pulled tight across your body. The amount of fat under the skin also reduces and the skin itself becomes thinner and drier, causing the top layer to weaken and form into folds.

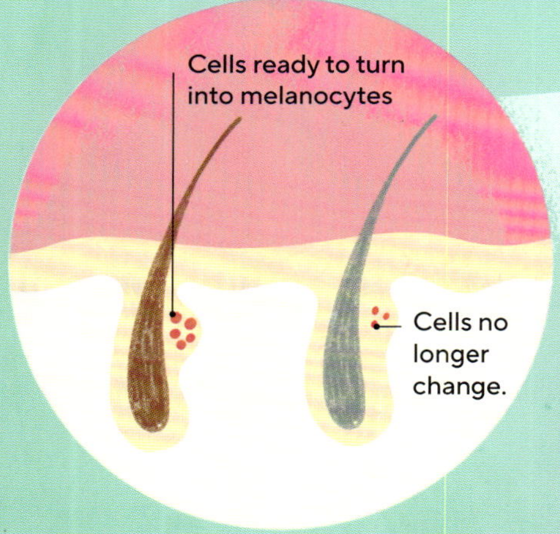

- Cells ready to turn into melanocytes
- Cells no longer change.

WHY DOES YOUR HAIR GO GREY AS YOU GET OLDER?

The colour of your hair is determined by pigment-producing cells called melanocytes. As you get older – or sometimes due to other reasons such as stress and genetics – you make fewer of these cells and the hair loses its colour.

WHAT MAKES YOU FART?

When bacteria break down food in your digestive system, they produce gases, which can be released from the body in little bursts through your anus. The smelliest farts contain a gas called hydrogen sulfide, nicknamed "rotten egg gas".

Why do you want dessert even when you are full?

Even when you are stuffed, your brain will still make you crave foods that have a lot of calories packed into a small space (such as those high in sugar and fat like cake). This is thought to be an ancient survival instinct to encourage our ancestors to make the most of energy sources when they found them.

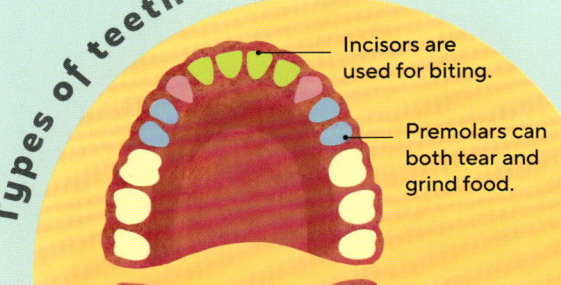

Types of teeth

- Incisors are used for biting.
- Premolars can both tear and grind food.
- Molars crush and grind food into a paste.
- Sharp canines can tear into food.

WHY ARE YOUR TEEETH DIFFERENT SHAPES?

By the time you are an adult you will have around 32 teeth, but they won't all look the same. At the front of your mouth are sharper teeth for biting into food and tearing it apart when it is tough. However, most of the chewing is done by teeth at the back of your mouth, which are flatter and perfectly placed to grind up each mouthful before it gets sent to your stomach.

WHAT HAPPENS WHEN YOU BLOW OUT CANDLES?

To extinguish little candle flames your body uses your abdominal muscles to push on your lungs and send air up your windpipe. You can seal your lips to temporarily hold the air in your mouth, and then expel it in one big puff. Compared to the air you breathe in, exhaled air contains less oxygen and more carbon dioxide (a waste product made by your cells), which helps smother the flames.

HEATWAVE

Soaking up the sun may be fun, but watch out you do not get too warm. Luckily, your body has many behind-the-scenes tricks to cool you down.

WHAT IS SWEAT MADE OF?
Sweat is mostly water and a tiny amount of salt. It is made deep in your skin by special cells (see page 35) and then travels upwards until it is released onto the surface of your skin at sites called pores. As heat is transferred from your body to the sweat, it evaporates from your skin, cooling your body.

Inside a tooth
- Hard dentine layer
- A tough coating called enamel protects the crown of the tooth.
- The middle of the tooth is soft pulp.
- Nerves and blood vessels extend into the gum.

WHY DO YOUR TEETH HURT WHEN YOU EAT ICE CREAM?
Your teeth are made of several layers – an outermost layer of enamel, followed by a layer of dentine and then the inner part of the tooth called the pulp. Lots of sensitive nerves are packed into the pulp. If the enamel erodes, the dentine is exposed and you may experience feelings of mild pain or sensitivity when you eat cold foods.

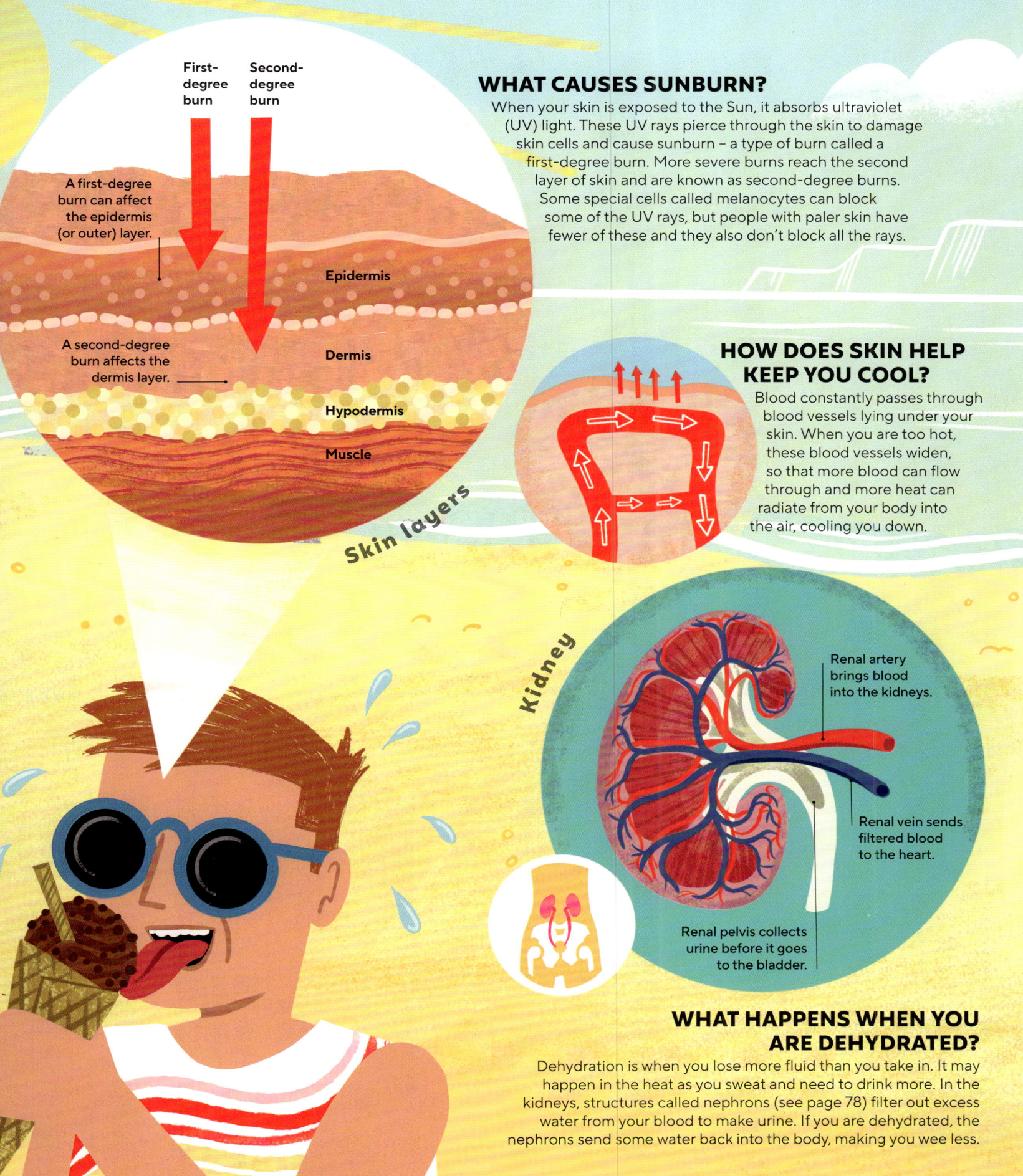

WHAT CAUSES SUNBURN?

When your skin is exposed to the Sun, it absorbs ultraviolet (UV) light. These UV rays pierce through the skin to damage skin cells and cause sunburn – a type of burn called a first-degree burn. More severe burns reach the second layer of skin and are known as second-degree burns. Some special cells called melanocytes can block some of the UV rays, but people with paler skin have fewer of these and they also don't block all the rays.

HOW DOES SKIN HELP KEEP YOU COOL?

Blood constantly passes through blood vessels lying under your skin. When you are too hot, these blood vessels widen, so that more blood can flow through and more heat can radiate from your body into the air, cooling you down.

WHAT HAPPENS WHEN YOU ARE DEHYDRATED?

Dehydration is when you lose more fluid than you take in. It may happen in the heat as you sweat and need to drink more. In the kidneys, structures called nephrons (see page 78) filter out excess water from your blood to make urine. If you are dehydrated, the nephrons send some water back into the body, making you wee less.

FLYING HIGH

While soaring through the sky at around 11 km (36,000 ft) above ground level, your body undergoes many temporary changes – from dulled taste buds to popping ears.

The middle ear

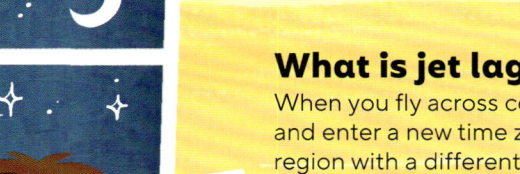

1. Ear canal has low-pressure air from the cabin after the plane has taken off.

2. Middle ear has high-pressure air from ground level trapped inside it.

3. The change in air pressure around the eardrum creates a popping sound.

4. When you yawn, air travels down the Eustachian tube and out of your throat, equalising the air pressure.

WHY DO YOUR EARS POP ON A PLANE?

There is always air trapped inside the ear, in the Eustachian tube behind the eardrum. Normally, this air pressure – the weight of the atmosphere pressing on you – matches the air pressure in the ear canal (see page 66). However, when you are in a plane that is taking off or landing, the air pressure in the cabin rapidly changes, faster than your Eustachian tube can adjust. This sudden air pressure difference causes a popping sound in your ear.

What is jet lag?

When you fly across countries and enter a new time zone – a region with a different time – it takes a while for your body to adjust. Your wake and sleep cycles are still in sync with your old time zone, so you may struggle to fall asleep when it gets dark. This sensation is called jet lag.

WHY DOES AEROPLANE FOOD TASTE DIFFERENT?

The dry air and low pressure in the plane cabin affects your taste buds, making them less sensitive to sweet and salty foods. The smell of food also affects its flavour (see page 105), and in the dry cabin air, the olfactory nerves in your nose are less effective. Together, your impaired sense of smell and taste means that food on a plane tastes more bland than usual!

- Brain combines information about smell and taste to create flavour.
- Olfactory bulb sends smell information to the brain.
- Olfactory nerves carry information about how a food smells to the olfactory bulb.
- Taste buds on the tongue detect whether a food is sweet, salty, sour, bitter, or umami.

Smell and taste

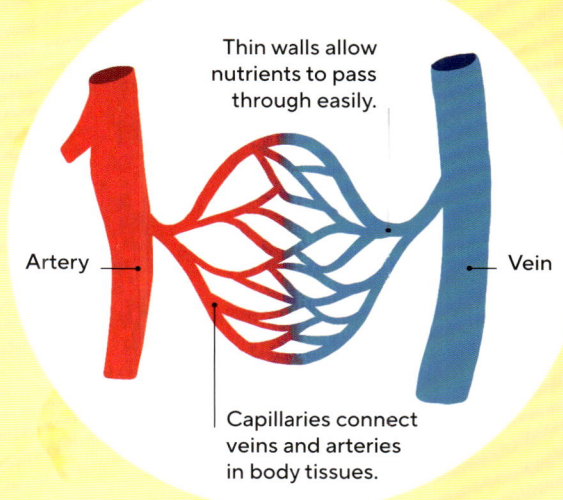

- Thin walls allow nutrients to pass through easily.
- Artery
- Vein
- Capillaries connect veins and arteries in body tissues.

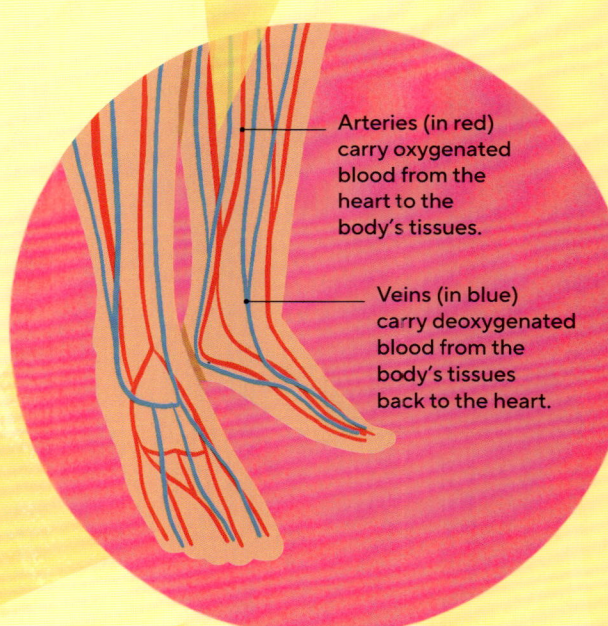

- Arteries (in red) carry oxygenated blood from the heart to the body's tissues.
- Veins (in blue) carry deoxygenated blood from the body's tissues back to the heart.

HOW IS BLOOD PUMPED UP AND DOWN YOUR BODY?

Even when you are sitting on a plane, the body's blood vessels – veins, arteries, and capillaries – are constantly moving blood throughout your body. Arteries carry blood to the body's tissues, while veins send blood back to the heart (see page 49). Capillaries are the tiniest blood vessels. With walls that are only one cell thick, they connect veins and arteries.

WINDING DOWN

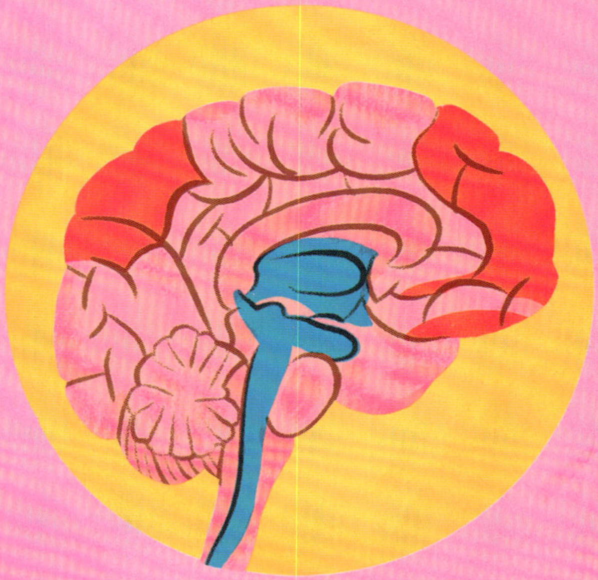

COOKING UP A STORM

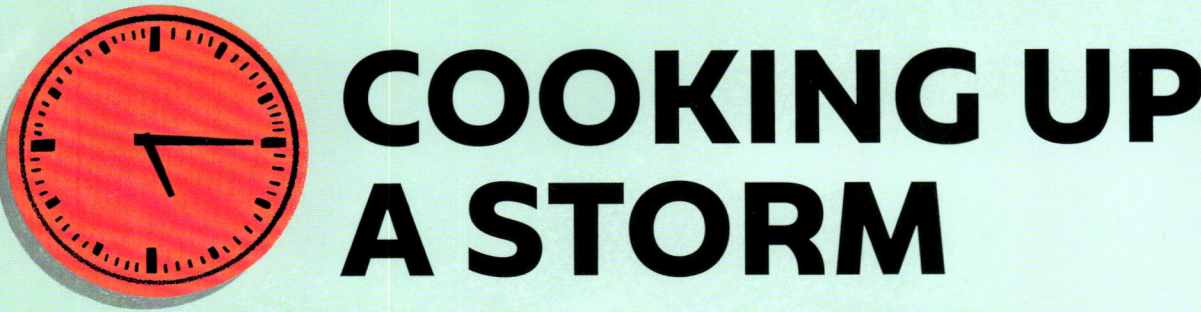

Your mouth may be watering, but dinner isn't ready yet. First your body must use fine motor skills to chop, slice, and dice every ingredient.

Reflex action

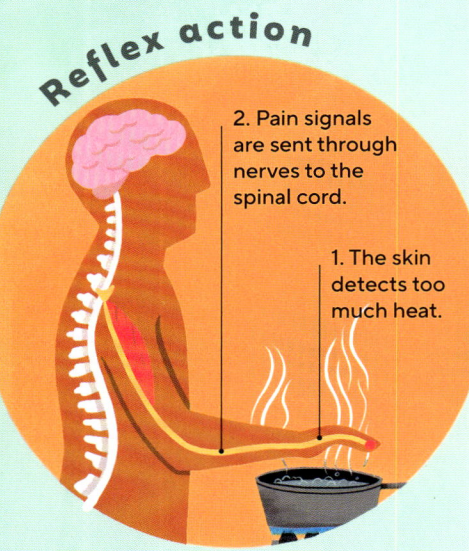

2. Pain signals are sent through nerves to the spinal cord.

1. The skin detects too much heat.

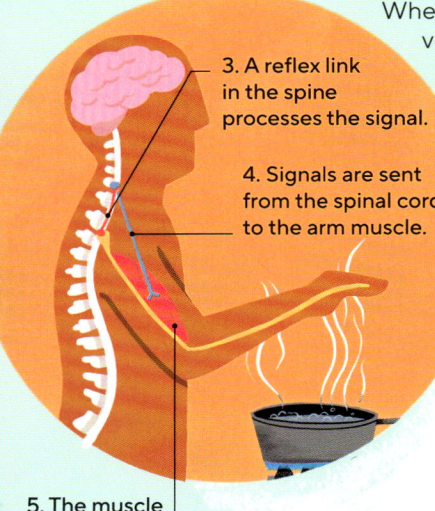

3. A reflex link in the spine processes the signal.

4. Signals are sent from the spinal cord to the arm muscle.

5. The muscle contracts to move the hand away.

WHAT IS A REFLEX ACTION?

When you accidentally touch something very hot, your body reacts almost instantly by pulling your hand away. This reaction is not coordinated by the brain, but instead by nerves in your spine. The pain signal travels to the spinal cord, which immediately tells your muscles to move away from the source of pain. Signals then reach the brain after this has taken place, so you don't feel the pain until slightly later.

Why do onions make you cry?

When an onion is chopped, the chemicals inside it begin to react – giving off an invisible gas that irritates your eyes. Glands around the eye then produce tears to wash away what has bothered the eyes.

Brain hemispheres

The right hemisphere controls the left side of the body.

The left hemisphere controls the right side of the body.

WHY DO YOU HAVE A DOMINANT HAND?

The majority of people around the world are right-handed, with only around 11 per cent having a dominant left hand. It used to be thought that a person's handedness matched which side of the brain they favoured, because each hemisphere (half) controls half of the body. But, while studies have found there are some brain differences between left-handers and right-handers, scientists still don't really know why most people prefer one hand over the other.

HOW DO YOU SENSE DIFFERENT TEXTURES?

The thick texture of ketchup is sensed by cells in the hand.

As you touch different objects, the grooves in your fingers pass over them. Inside these grooves are tiny cells called sensory neurons. Part of the nervous system, these cells collect information about what you have touched – whether it is hard or soft, hot or cold – and transmit this through the body to the brain.

WHY DO YOU HAVE FINGERPRINTS?

Every person has unique fingerprints – even identical twins! Scientists used to think that the swirling patterns of lines on our fingertips helped us to grip objects, but now they think these are used more in sensing items.

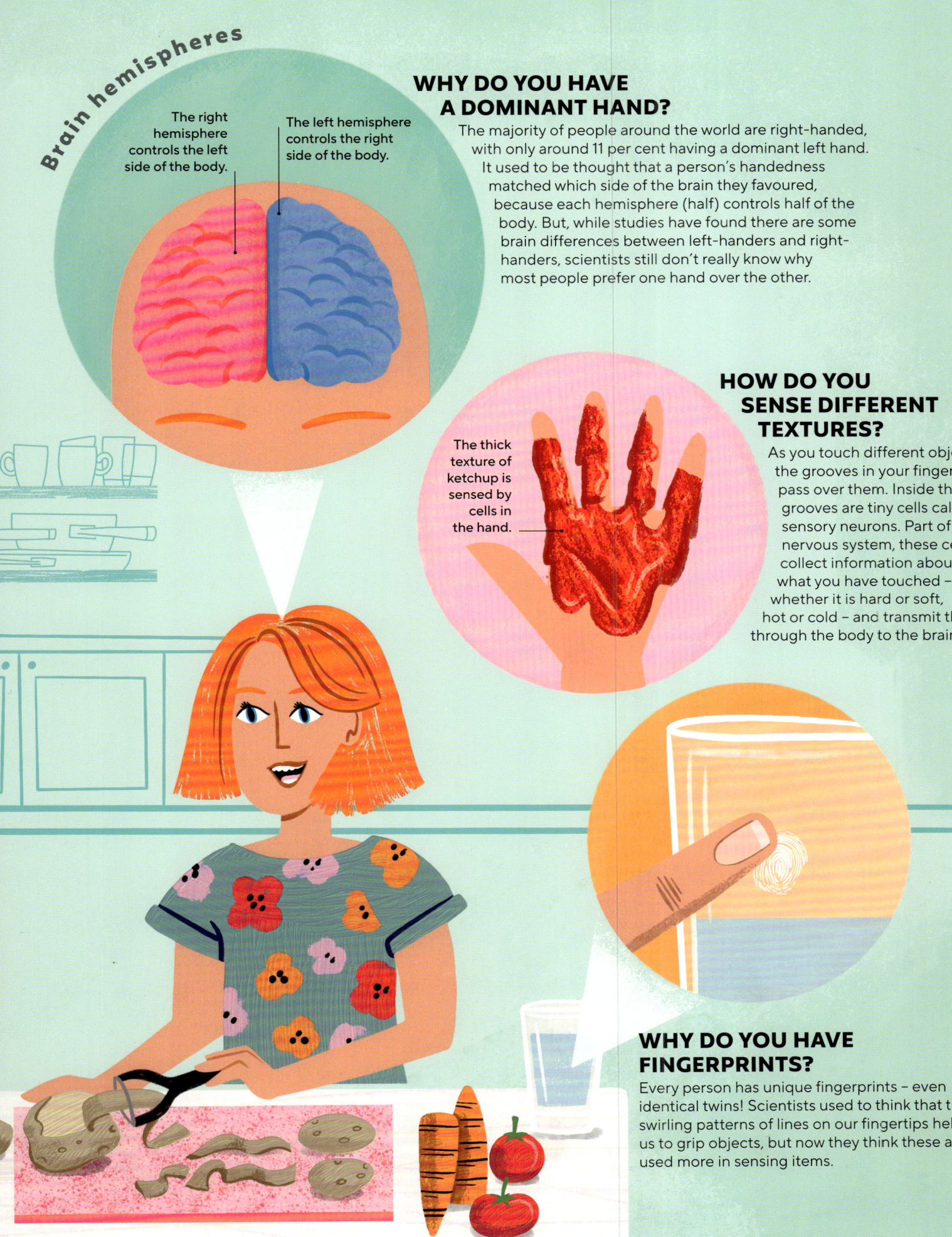

101

What is happening in your brain when you feel happy?

Your brain releases feel-good hormones – dopamine, serotonin, endorphins, and oxytocin – into your bloodstream when you do something that makes you feel happy. These chemical messengers help to regulate your mood, promote feelings of pleasure and motivation, and give you a sense of wellbeing.

Is it true that laughing is good for you?

Yes! There are many positive effects associated with laughing. These range from taking in more oxygen-rich air and stimulating muscles around the body, to boosting your mood and reducing your stress levels.

What makes people feel happy?

Everyone has unique things that make them feel joyful. Some people feel happy when spending quality time with people whose company they enjoy, such as family, friends, or a pet, while others prefer to spend time alone or doing a special hobby. Happiness can also come from a goal you've achieved or from new, exciting, or relaxing experiences such as holidays.

Why do you laugh?

Humans laugh as an emotional and physical response to different things. Many people laugh when they feel happy or when they find something funny, but it is also very common to laugh when nervous. Laughing also helps us to connect, bond, and relax with the people around us.

Why is laughter contagious?

In a similar way to yawning (see pages 10–11) laughing is contagious because humans are built to copy each other's behaviour. When we see or hear someone else laughing, our brain uses this sensory information and tells us to laugh too, and the shared laughter makes us feel even happier!

FEELING HAPPY

Laughing and feeling joyful are an important part of life. Whether it is the playful antics of your pets or fun with friends that makes you happy, sources of this positive emotion are all around us.

EAT UP

Munching and chewing might be messy, but using your mouth to turn food into mush is where the long process of digestion begins.

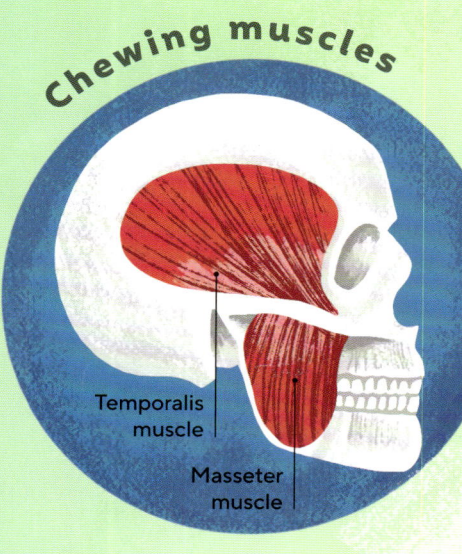

Chewing muscles

Temporalis muscle
Masseter muscle

WHY DO YOU NEED TO CHEW YOUR FOOD?

Mastication – or chewing – breaks food down into more manageable pieces. Strong muscles in the face move your jaw up and down, allowing your teeth to grind food into a pulp that is easier to swallow.

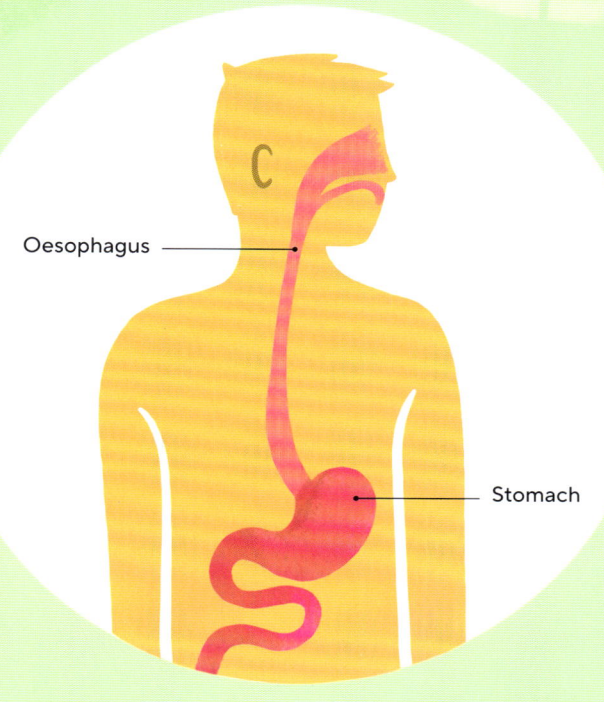

Oesophagus

Stomach

WHERE DOES SPIT COME FROM?

Nerve signals, including some from the facial nerve, trigger special salivary glands in the face to produce saliva, or spit. This is released through ducts into the mouth. As well as helping to moisten food so that it is easier to swallow, saliva contains chemical substances that begin to break it down.

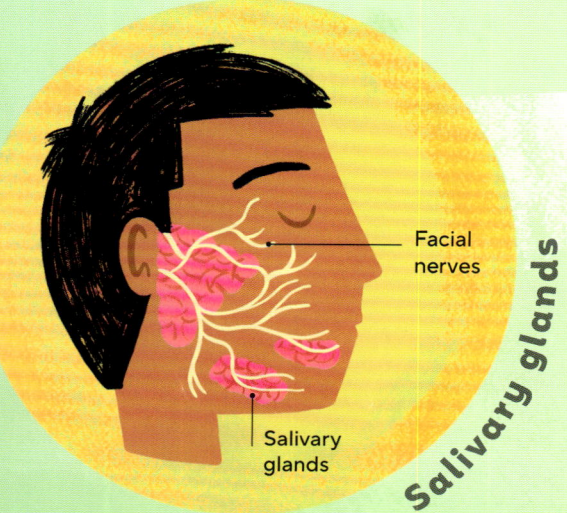

Facial nerves

Salivary glands

Salivary glands

WHERE DOES FOOD GO?

After leaving your mouth, food travels down a long tube called the oesophagus. Muscles in the wall of this tube squeeze to push food downwards to the stomach. Thanks to this process – called peristalsis – you can eat standing on your head (although doctors advise you not to try this)!

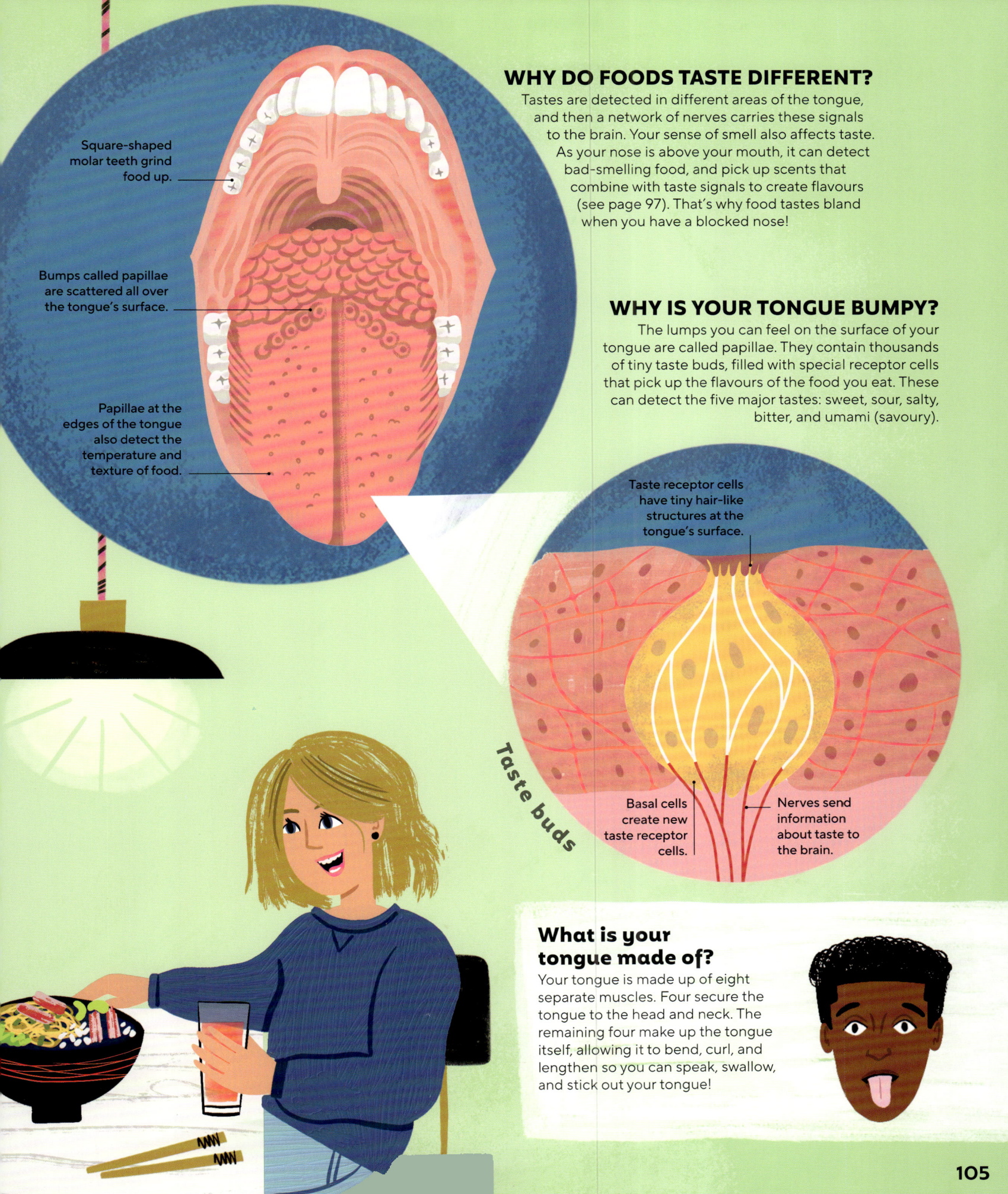

- Square-shaped molar teeth grind food up.
- Bumps called papillae are scattered all over the tongue's surface.
- Papillae at the edges of the tongue also detect the temperature and texture of food.

WHY DO FOODS TASTE DIFFERENT?

Tastes are detected in different areas of the tongue, and then a network of nerves carries these signals to the brain. Your sense of smell also affects taste. As your nose is above your mouth, it can detect bad-smelling food, and pick up scents that combine with taste signals to create flavours (see page 97). That's why food tastes bland when you have a blocked nose!

WHY IS YOUR TONGUE BUMPY?

The lumps you can feel on the surface of your tongue are called papillae. They contain thousands of tiny taste buds, filled with special receptor cells that pick up the flavours of the food you eat. These can detect the five major tastes: sweet, sour, salty, bitter, and umami (savoury).

Taste buds

- Taste receptor cells have tiny hair-like structures at the tongue's surface.
- Basal cells create new taste receptor cells.
- Nerves send information about taste to the brain.

What is your tongue made of?

Your tongue is made up of eight separate muscles. Four secure the tongue to the head and neck. The remaining four make up the tongue itself, allowing it to bend, curl, and lengthen so you can speak, swallow, and stick out your tongue!

105

TIME TO DIGEST

Your meal may be over, but inside you each mini morsel still has far to travel. As you wash up, your food is washed down – deep into your digestive system.

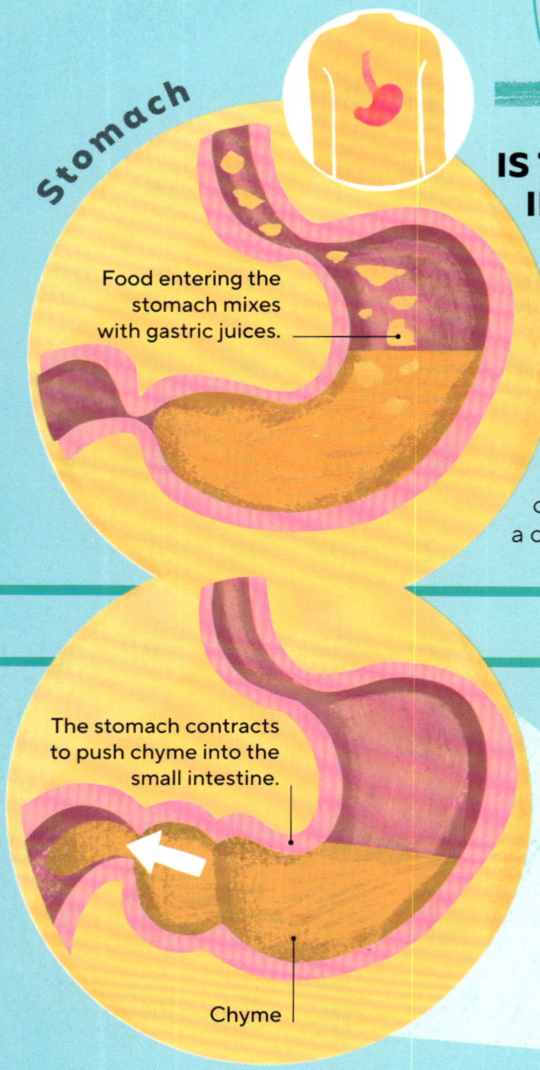

Stomach

Food entering the stomach mixes with gastric juices.

The stomach contracts to push chyme into the small intestine.

Chyme

IS THERE REALLY ACID IN YOUR STOMACH?

After travelling down your throat, the first place food reaches is the large squishy bag of your stomach. Here it mixes with gastric juices so strong and acidic that they begin to break it down. Over a period of several hours, food gets crushed and churned into a creamy liquid called chyme.

WHY DOES YOUR BELLY SOMETIMES MAKE NOISES WHEN DIGESTING?

Food doesn't slide neatly through your digestive system. It is pushed along by strong muscles in the organs that make up the digestive tract (see page 64), which can be quite noisy! These send partially digested food (chyme) from the stomach to the small intestine. In this long organ, nutrients are extracted from food and passed into the bloodstream.

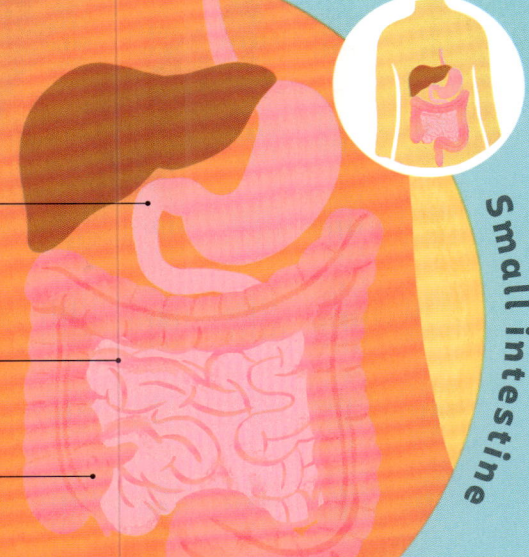

1. Food enters the small intestine from the stomach.
2. The middle section of the intestine is where most digestion takes place.
3. Food then enters the large intestine.

Small intestine

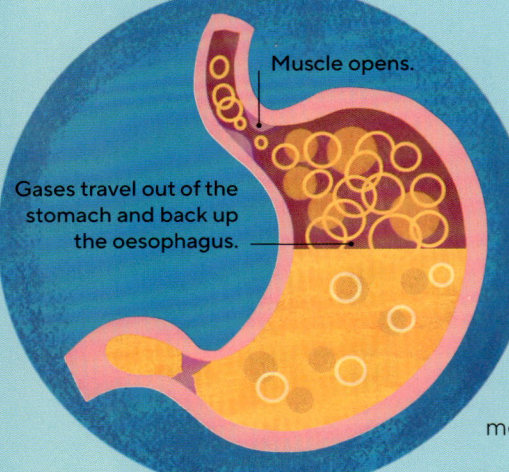

Muscle opens.

Gases travel out of the stomach and back up the oesophagus.

WHY DO YOU BURP?

As you drink and eat, you may accidentally take in excess air. This expands the stomach, causing the muscle at the top of the stomach to open up, so gas can pass back up the oesophagus and out of your mouth in a little pop.

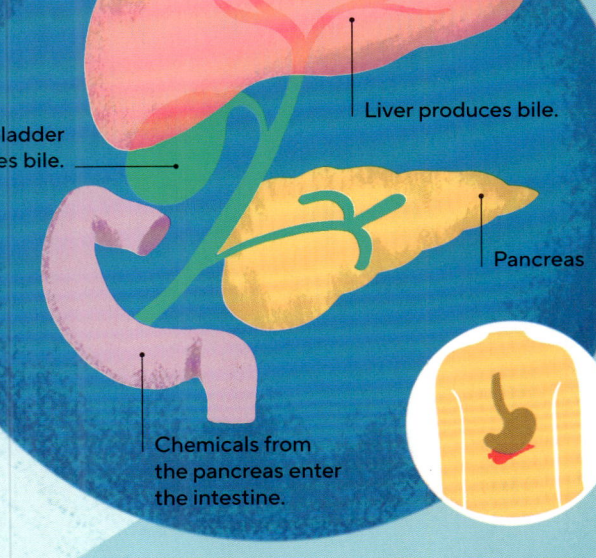

Pancreas

Liver produces bile.

Gallbladder stores bile.

Pancreas

Chemicals from the pancreas enter the intestine.

HOW DOES FOOD GET BROKEN DOWN?

Most of the chemicals needed to digest food are produced in an organ called the pancreas and then sent to the small intestine through small ducts. Called enzymes, these chemicals target specific foods and break them into simpler substances. The liver also produces a liquid called bile, which helps to digest fats.

Zooming Out

There are lots of different types of gut bacteria. But where in the body are they found?

SOME BACTERIA CAN SWIM TENS OF TIMES THEIR BODY LENGTH IN JUST ONE SECOND!

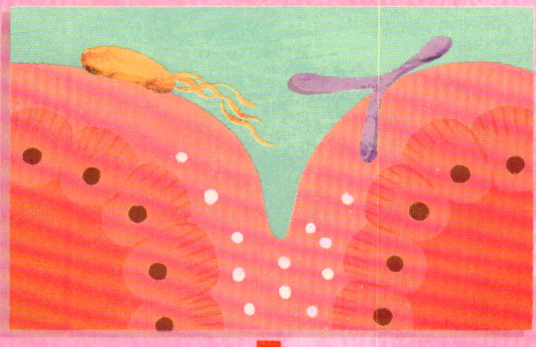

A lining made of cells...
The lining of the large intestine, located in the abdomen, is home to different types of bacteria such as E. coli.

...to tissue...
Layers of tissue and muscle line the large intestines. They absorb water from food waste and propel food along.

...to organs...
The large intestine turns waste products into poo, which is then excreted. When stretched out, the intestine is around 1.5 m (5 ft) long.

A tail called a flagellum helps the bacterium swim through the large intestine.

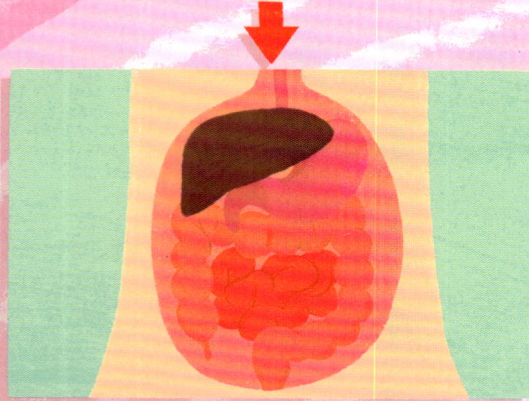

...to body systems
The organs that make up the digestive system (see page 129) work together to move food through the body, breaking it down into nutrients that can be absorbed.

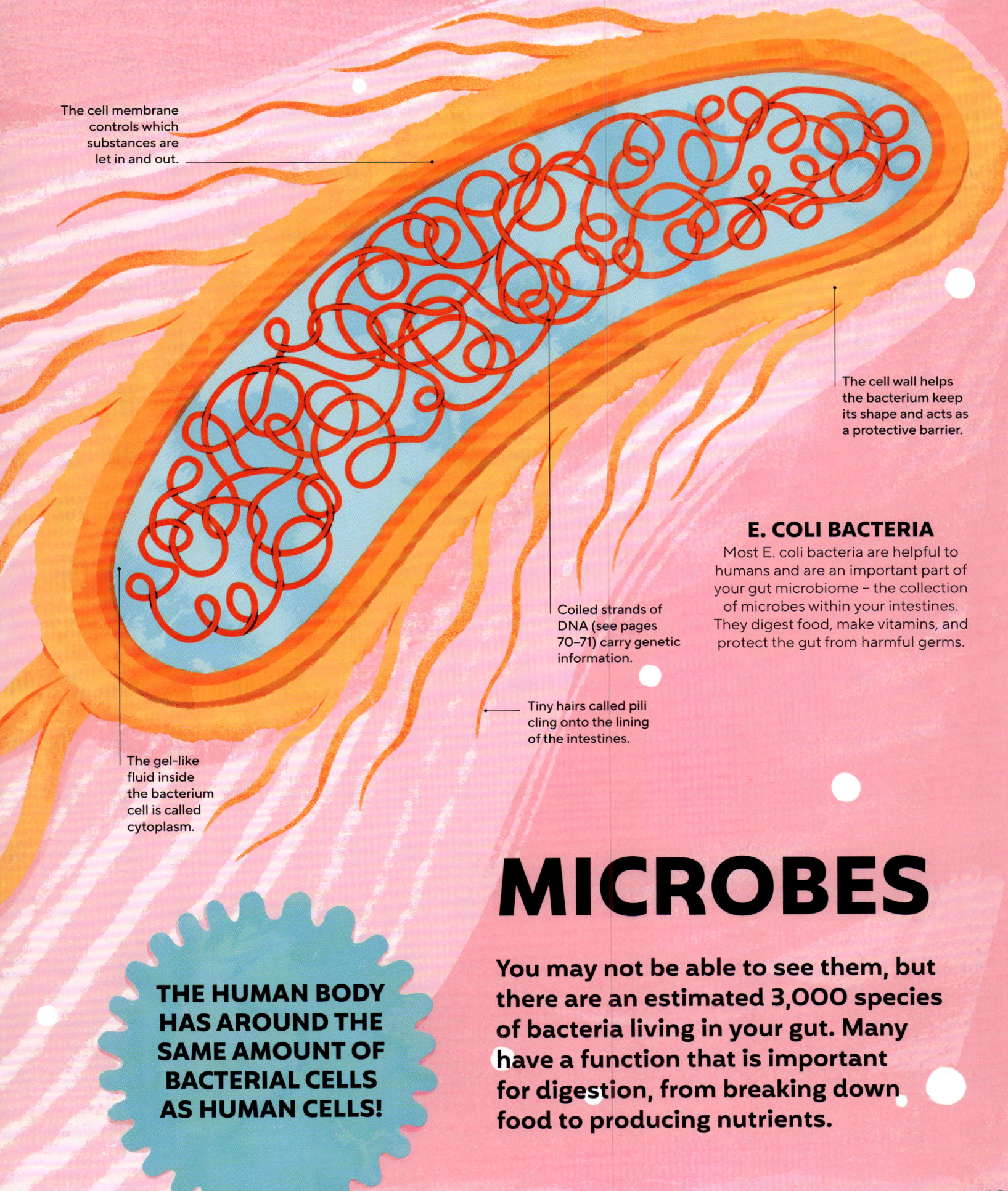

The cell membrane controls which substances are let in and out.

The cell wall helps the bacterium keep its shape and acts as a protective barrier.

Coiled strands of DNA (see pages 70–71) carry genetic information.

Tiny hairs called pili cling onto the lining of the intestines.

The gel-like fluid inside the bacterium cell is called cytoplasm.

E. COLI BACTERIA

Most E. coli bacteria are helpful to humans and are an important part of your gut microbiome – the collection of microbes within your intestines. They digest food, make vitamins, and protect the gut from harmful germs.

MICROBES

You may not be able to see them, but there are an estimated 3,000 species of bacteria living in your gut. Many have a function that is important for digestion, from breaking down food to producing nutrients.

THE HUMAN BODY HAS AROUND THE SAME AMOUNT OF BACTERIAL CELLS AS HUMAN CELLS!

GAME ON!

Staring at the screen is not always bad for you. Fending off foes in a game keeps your brain cells busy, and can improve your hand-eye coordination, decision-making, and memory.

HOW DOES YOUR BRAIN PROCESS SO MUCH INFORMATION?

The outer layer of your brain is known as the cerebral cortex. Its wrinkly appearance is created by folds and grooves, which give it a huge surface area packed with lots of nerve cells. This vast amount of cells and the many connections between them allow the brain to assess large amounts of information and to learn, reason, and solve problems.

Cerebral cortex

The cortex is 3–5 mm (0.1–0.2 in) thick.

Each nerve cell has many branching filaments, allowing it to connect with lots of others.

HOW DO BRAIN CELLS WORK?

The brain contains around 86 billion nerve cells. These specialized cells have long branches that extend out from the central cell body to connect with other cells. Where the branches meet, electrical impulses pass across the gaps between them. These exchanges of information generate your thoughts and actions.

Brain cells

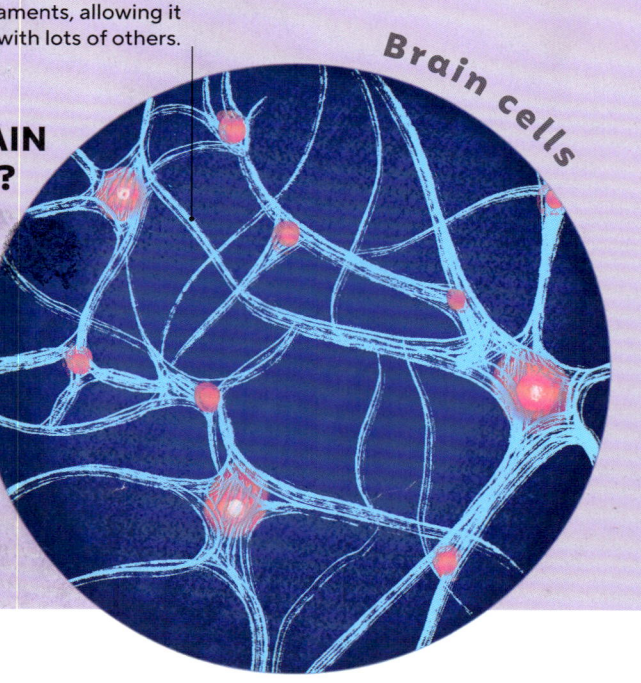

Layers of the eye

- Jelly-filled chamber
- The protective outer layer (sclera) is known as the white of the eye.
- Cornea protects the iris and the pupil.
- Pupil
- Iris, the coloured part of the eye
- Lens, a disc of transparent tissue
- Retina, a layer holding light-sensitive cells

WHAT IS INSIDE YOUR EYES?

The squishy ball of your eye is filled with a thick jelly-like fluid that holds its shape, protected by a tough outer coating. As light enters through the pupil, it passes through both a clear cornea and a lens, which focus the light (see pages 38–39). The innermost layer of the eye – called the retina – contains light-detecting cells, which capture the image coming in from your screen.

HOW DO YOU GET BETTER AT GAMING?

The more you play video games, the faster your hands are able to move over the controller and switch between buttons. Your reaction times and reflexes improve by repetition of a task, as the pathways between nerve cells in the brain are reinforced. This makes it quicker and easier for your brain to carry out the task again.

Does looking at screens make it harder to sleep?

Your body wakes and sleeps in a regular cycle known as its circadian rhythm, which is influenced by when it goes dark outside. Screens emit blue light waves, just like the Sun. If you stare at a screen at night, your brain might think it is still daytime, and not release the hormones that make you sleepy, keeping you awake.

THE BODY AT HIGH SPEED

Do you feel the need for speed? When accelerating and moving extremely fast, the body experiences strong gravitational forces known as G-forces. Among the many effects of such serious speed, higher G-forces can cause the blood to feel heavier, making it harder for the heart to pump it to the brain. Hold on tight!

THE **EXCITEMENT** OF TRAVELLING AT HIGH SPEEDS CAN TRIGGER THE RELEASE OF **ENDORPHINS**, CHEMICAL SIGNALS THAT DULL PAIN AND PRODUCE A SENSE OF **EUPHORIA**.

G-FORCE CAN ACT ON **THE SKIN**, PULLING IT BACK AND MAKING FACES LOOK DISTORTED.

WHEN G-FORCES ARE HIGH, BLOOD MAY STRUGGLE TO REACH THE **RETINA OF THE EYE**, CAUSING **TUNNEL VISION** WHERE YOU CAN SEE LESS ON EACH SIDE.

WHEN HANGING **UPSIDE DOWN**, THE INCREASED BLOOD FLOW TO THE HEAD CAN MAKE THE SINUSES FEEL **CONGESTED**.

WHEN YOU PLUNGE DOWNWARDS THE **STOMACH** MOVES **UPWARDS** RELATIVE TO THE REST OF THE BODY, CREATING THE SENSATION OF **WEIGHTLESSNESS**.

ON A **ROLLERCOASTER** YOU MIGHT EXPERIENCE 3 G, BUT SPECIALLY TRAINED **PILOTS** CAN WITHSTAND EVEN MORE G-FORCE – **UP TO 9 G!**

AT **EXTREME G-FORCES** THE HEART MAY NOT BE ABLE TO PUMP ENOUGH BLOOD TO THE BRAIN, WHICH CAN LEAD TO YOU **PASS OUT!**

STUNT PILOTS PREPARING FOR HIGH G-FORCES **TENSE THEIR MUSCLES** AND BREATHE RHYTHMICALLY TO **MAINTAIN BLOOD FLOW** TO THE UPPER BODY AND BRAIN.

ANTI-G-FORCE FLIGHT SUITS HAVE **INFLATABLE SACS** IN THE LOWER BODY THAT PREVENT BLOOD FROM BEING FORCED DOWNWARDS. THIS MAINTAINS **BLOOD PRESSURE** IN THE UPPER BODY.

SLEEPOVER

Whether it's braiding hair or painting nails, playing with your appearance can be fun. But what makes up your fingers, face, and hairy head?

Nail structure

- The tissue under the nail is called the nail matrix.
- Nail plate
- Nail bone (phalanx)

HOW FAST DO YOUR NAILS GROW?

Fingernails grow by an average of 0.1 mm (0.003 in) per day. A layer of tissue beneath the base of the nail produces cells that form the newest-growing part of the fingernail. The new cells push the older ones forwards, making the nail appear to lengthen from the tip.

Hair follicles

- Round follicles produce straight hair.
- Elliptical-shaped follicles produce coiled hair.

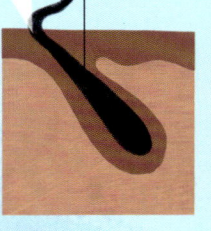
Curly hairs come out of the skin at an angle.

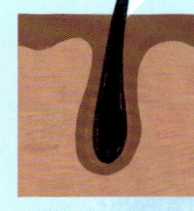
Straight hairs grow upright.

WHY DO SOME PEOPLE HAVE CURLY HAIR AND OTHERS HAVE STRAIGHT HAIR?

The hair type we have is one of many factors passed on by genes from our parents. It is determined by the shape of the follicles – the tiny holes on our head that individual hairs sprout from. People with tightly curled hair have more oval-shaped follicles, while those with straighter hair have rounder follicles.

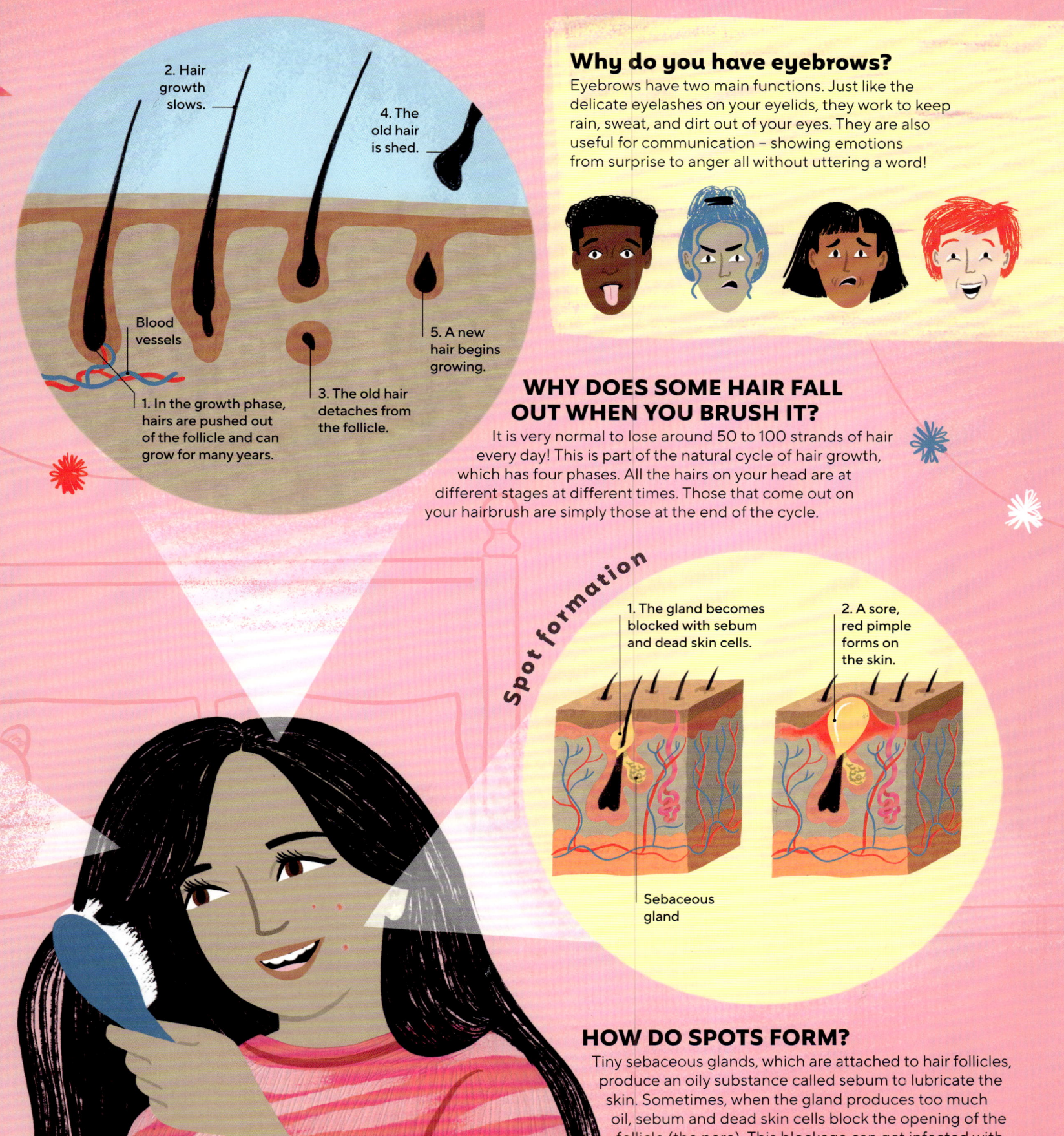

Why do you have eyebrows?
Eyebrows have two main functions. Just like the delicate eyelashes on your eyelids, they work to keep rain, sweat, and dirt out of your eyes. They are also useful for communication – showing emotions from surprise to anger all without uttering a word!

WHY DOES SOME HAIR FALL OUT WHEN YOU BRUSH IT?
It is very normal to lose around 50 to 100 strands of hair every day! This is part of the natural cycle of hair growth, which has four phases. All the hairs on your head are at different stages at different times. Those that come out on your hairbrush are simply those at the end of the cycle.

Spot formation
1. The gland becomes blocked with sebum and dead skin cells.
2. A sore, red pimple forms on the skin.

Sebaceous gland

HOW DO SPOTS FORM?
Tiny sebaceous glands, which are attached to hair follicles, produce an oily substance called sebum to lubricate the skin. Sometimes, when the gland produces too much oil, sebum and dead skin cells block the opening of the follicle (the pore). This blockage can get infected with bacteria and cause a bumpy, oozy spot or pimple on the surface of the skin.

ON YOUR SKIN

From birthmarks to freckles, everyone has features on their skin that make them unique. But while many are perfectly harmless, some need to be monitored for any changes.

FRECKLES

These small red or brown spots are caused by an overproduction of melanin – pigment cells that give colour to our skin, hair, and eyes – from being in the sun. Freckles often appear in areas that are frequently exposed, such as the face or arms. People are not born with freckles – they typically develop in childhood, and can fade or even disappear as a person grows older. Anyone can have freckles, but they are more common in people with fair skin and hair.

ACNE

Acne is a common skin condition that causes persistent pimples and oily skin. It happens when hair follicles become clogged with oil and dead cells, and get infected with bacteria (see page 115). Teenagers are more likely to have acne due to hormone changes during puberty, but anyone can be affected. If acne becomes a problem that affects your daily life, do see a doctor for treatment.

MOLES

Round, coloured growths are called moles. Typically larger than a freckle, they develop when pigment cells called melanocytes grow on the skin in clusters. Although most moles are harmless, it's important to speak to a doctor if you spot any changes in a mole's shape, size, or colouring.

Clusters of sore, recurring spots form acne.

Moles can be raised and bumpy but some are flat, too.

WARTS AND VERRUCAS

Warts are small lumps on the skin. When they are on the sole of the foot, warts are sometimes called verrucas. They are caused by a virus that makes the skin's top layer produce too much keratin (a type of protein), and this later forms a wart. They are contagious and can be spread by skin to skin contact, or by sharing towels or walking on wet floors in communal changing rooms.

Warts are rough, hard, and bumpy in texture.

BIRTHMARKS

These areas of coloured skin may appear when you are born or very soon after. Some birthmarks are caused by blood vessels that do not form properly, while other birthmarks appear when pigment cells grow in groups. They vary widely in their appearance – birthmarks can be small, brown, and flat, or raised and red, stretching across the face. Some birthmarks gradually shrink and disappear over time.

SLEEP TIGHT

At the end of the day, snuggling down under the covers can make you nod off to sleep. Your body will rest and recharge, but never stops working.

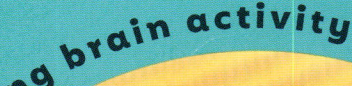

Sleeping brain activity

- Movement control is turned off as this area is at rest.
- The area responsible for reasoning is not active.
- Visual cortex generates images.
- The amygdala is active, generating emotions.
- Brainstem controls the switch between sleep and waking.

IS THE BRAIN ASLEEP WHILE YOU SLEEP?

Brain waves slow down as you fall into a slumber, but many parts of the brain are still active. During the stage of sleep when you dream, areas that involve emotions and imagery show higher levels of activity. The areas that deal with reasoning, movement, and awareness of the space around you are inactive.

Why do you dream?

Although we spend so much time dreaming, experts are not sure why this is! Some think dreams could be a way we form or work through memories. Others believe they help the brain to process emotions and information. But it is possible that dreams serve no function at all.

WHY DO SOME PEOPLE SNORE?

When you sleep, your muscles relax. The soft parts at the back of the mouth, including the tongue and the flap that separates your nose and throat, go floppy. As air passes over them, they vibrate, which can sometimes generate sound waves that come out as a loud rumbling noise! There are many reasons some people snore more than others, such as age or the shape of their throat.

Muscles relax and tissues vibrate as air passes over.

Air is drawn in.

Sound comes from mouth and nose.

Snoring

Why do you sometimes wake up in the middle of the night?

Not all sleep is the same. Your body actually cycles between three different stages: light sleep, deep sleep, and a stage called REM (rapid eye movement). In periods of light sleep, you might wake up, but almost nothing will wake a person in deep sleep. You dream during REM sleep. The graph below shows an example of sleep cycles through the night.

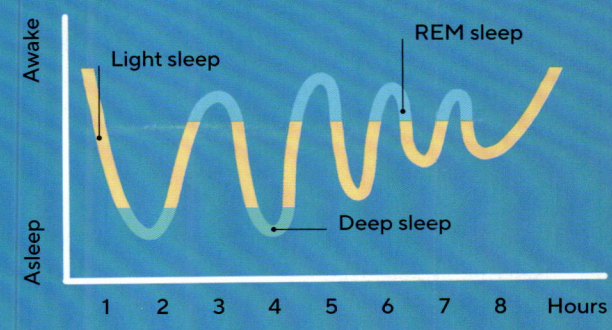

Chambers of the heart

The aorta (an artery) carries blood full of oxygen to organs and tissues.

Veins carry blood back to the heart.

Oxygen-poor blood is pumped up to the lungs.

Oxygen-poor blood from the body flows into the right atrium.

Oxygen-rich blood from the lungs enters the heart.

Valves between the chambers make sure blood only flows one way.

The left ventricle receives oxygen-rich blood from the left atrium.

The right ventricle receives oxygen-poor blood from the right atrium.

DOES YOUR HEART REST WHILE YOU SLEEP?

While your heart slows down slightly when you sleep, it never stops pumping. The heart is made up of four different chambers, each surrounded by walls of tough cardiac muscle. Every time the heart pumps, these muscles squeeze – pushing blood received from veins through each of these chambers and back out through arteries to the body. Some goes to your body's organs and tissues, while other blood goes to the lungs to pick up oxygen, in a process called double circulation (see pages 48–49).

GROWING UP

All through the day and even when you sleep your body keeps growing. You can expect to shoot up in size through your teens, with growth not fully stopping until your twenties.

Why do babies have such big heads?

A newborn's head can look massive compared their body – making up more than ¼ of their height! This proportionally big head is needed so that a baby's developing brain has space to rapidly grow in early life. When you finish growing, your head is about ⅛ of your height.

DO YOU GROW MORE WHILE YOU SLEEP?

No, but when you sleep a higher level of growth hormone is released from a small pea-sized part of the brain called the pituitary gland. As well as making you grow, this hormone triggers the repair of body tissues, more of which takes place at night when you are resting.

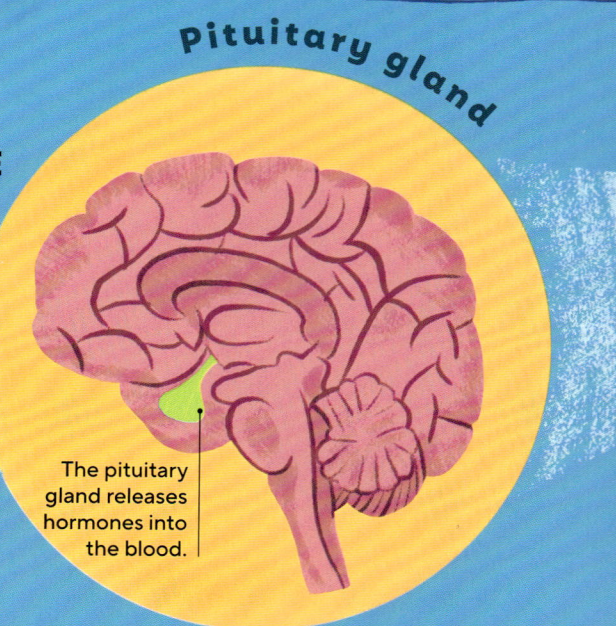

Pituitary gland

The pituitary gland releases hormones into the blood.

WHAT MAKES YOU GROW?

You began life as a single cell. This then splits into two identical cells, and then each of those divides into two more – eventually turning you from a small bundle of cells into a full body made of trillions! This process of cell division keeps going throughout your life, not only to make you grow, but also to replace damaged cells with new ones.

Cell division

1. Every cell has a nucleus, where DNA (genetic material) is stored.

2. A parent cell begins to duplicate the genetic material in its nucleus to make two sets.

3. During cell division, the parent cell splits in two.

4. Each of the resulting cells has the same DNA as the parent cell.

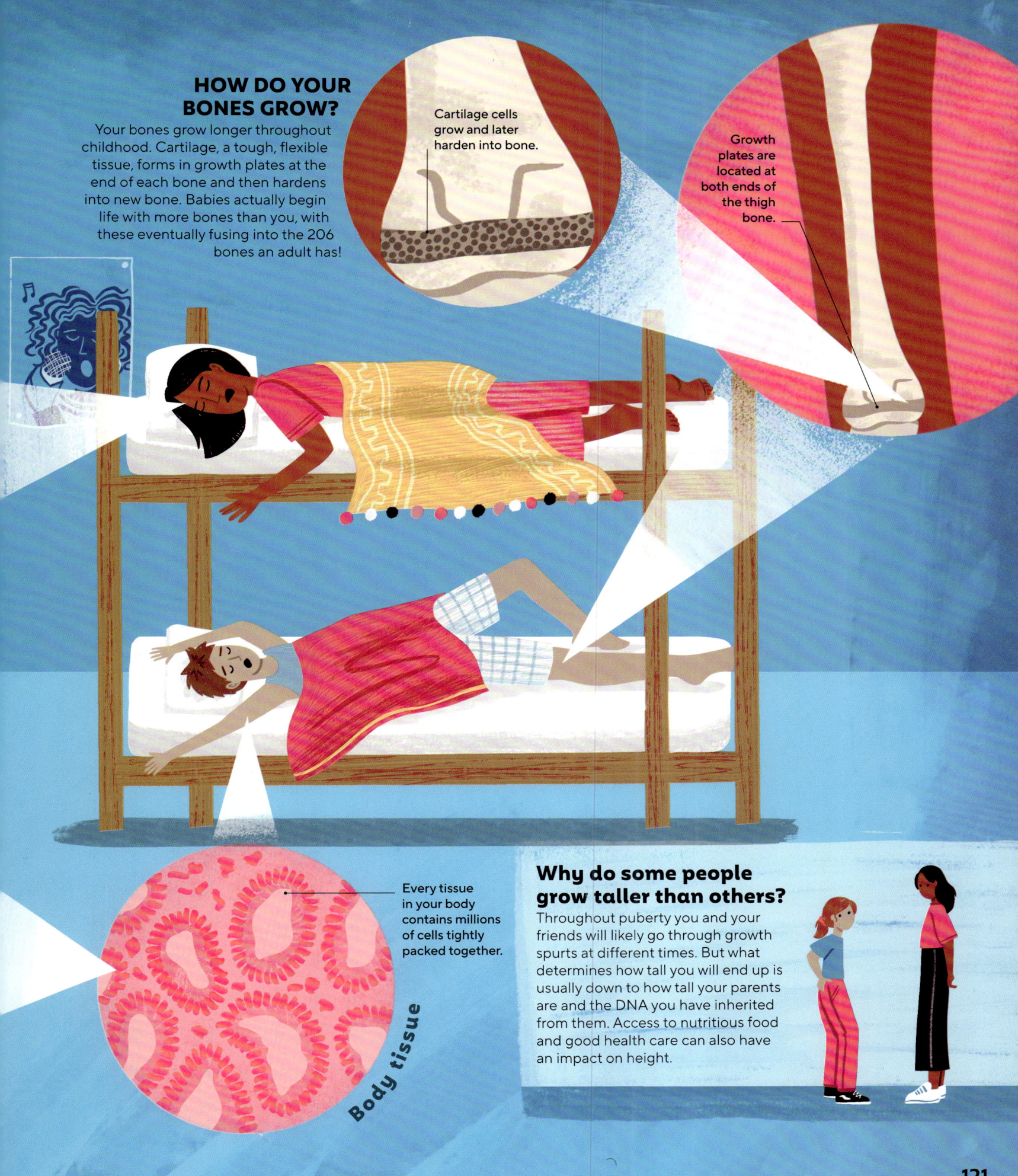

HOW DO YOUR BONES GROW?

Your bones grow longer throughout childhood. Cartilage, a tough, flexible tissue, forms in growth plates at the end of each bone and then hardens into new bone. Babies actually begin life with more bones than you, with these eventually fusing into the 206 bones an adult has!

Cartilage cells grow and later harden into bone.

Growth plates are located at both ends of the thigh bone.

Every tissue in your body contains millions of cells tightly packed together.

Body tissue

Why do some people grow taller than others?

Throughout puberty you and your friends will likely go through growth spurts at different times. But what determines how tall you will end up is usually down to how tall your parents are and the DNA you have inherited from them. Access to nutritious food and good health care can also have an impact on height.

BODY SYSTEMS

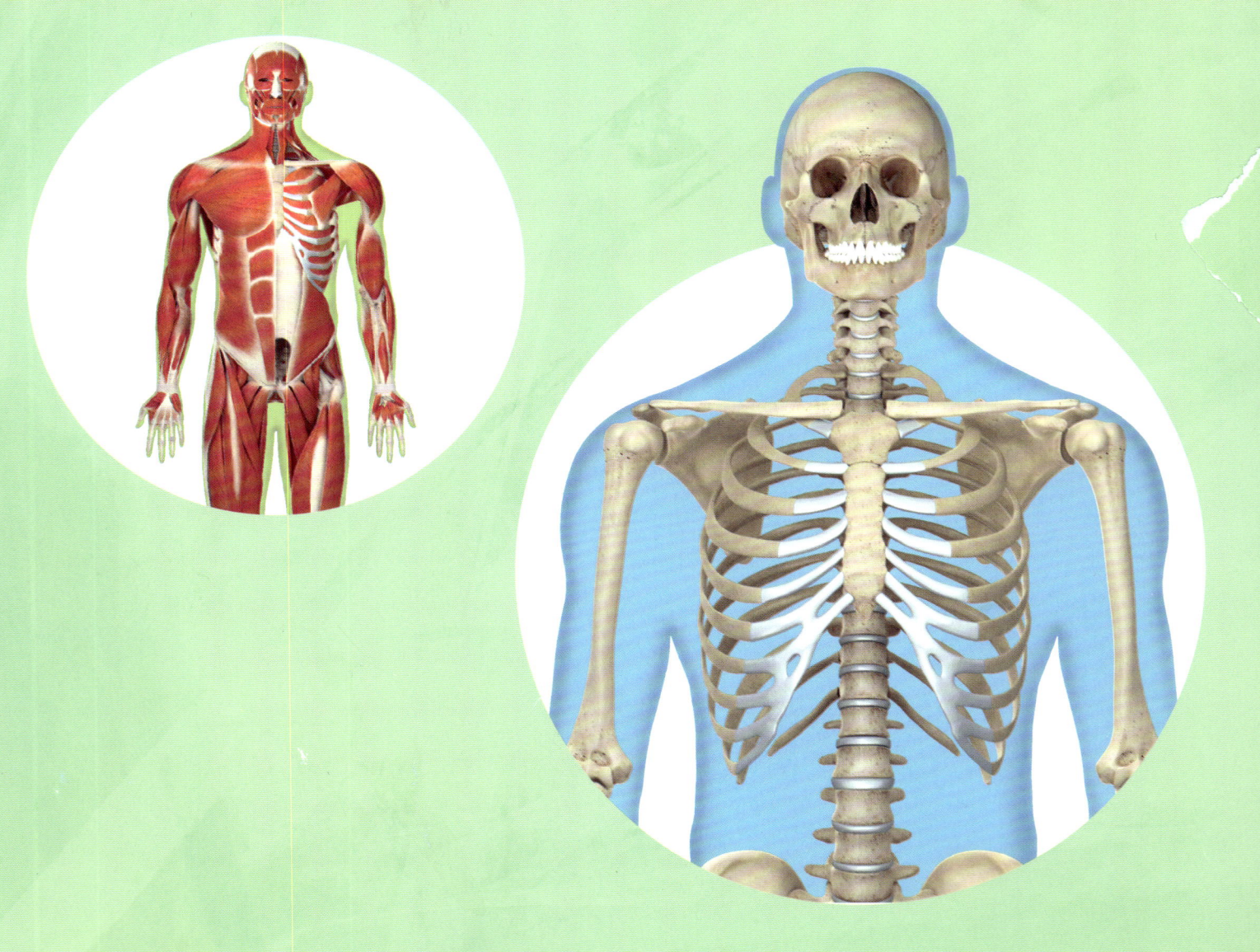

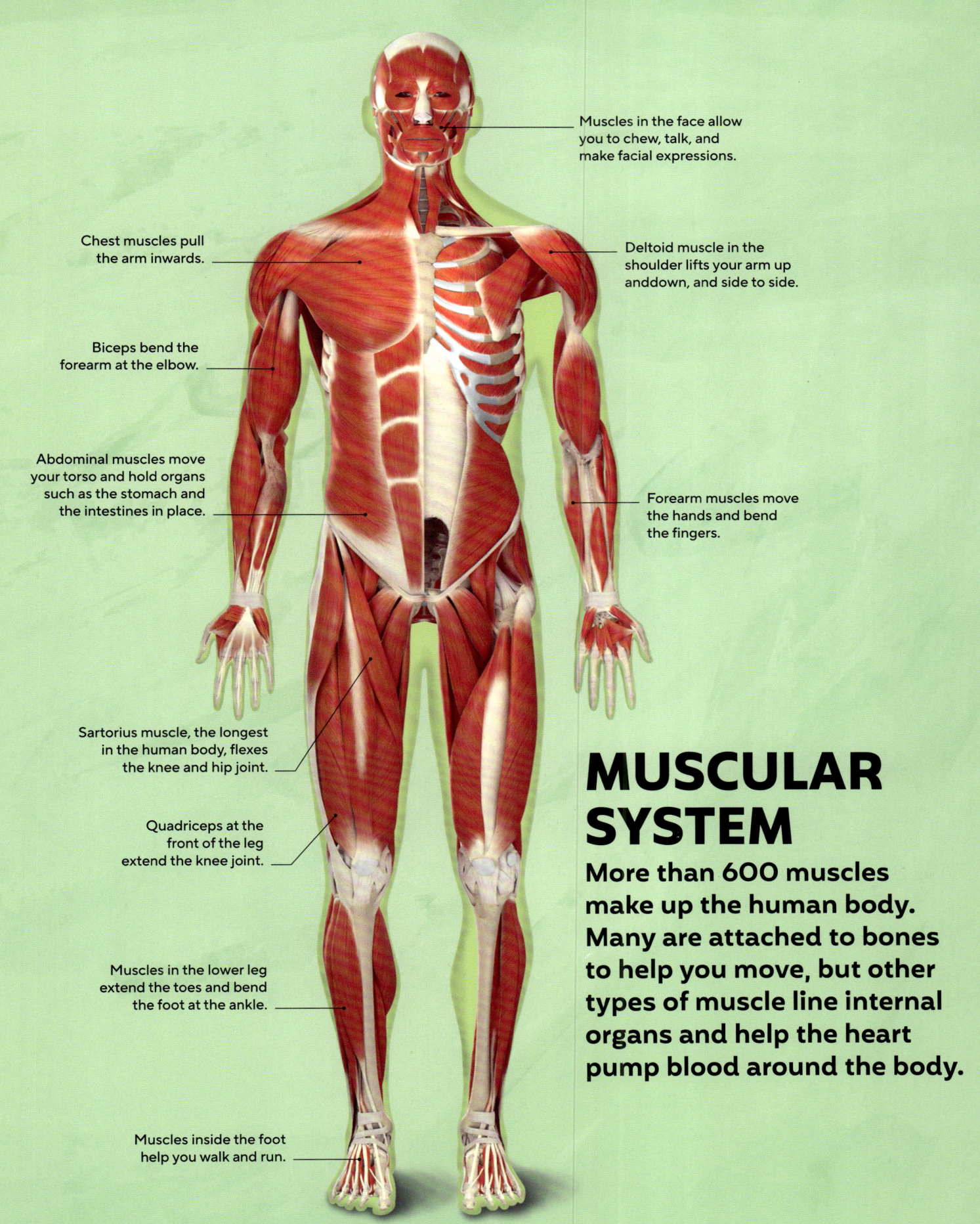

Muscles in the face allow you to chew, talk, and make facial expressions.

Chest muscles pull the arm inwards.

Deltoid muscle in the shoulder lifts your arm up and down, and side to side.

Biceps bend the forearm at the elbow.

Abdominal muscles move your torso and hold organs such as the stomach and the intestines in place.

Forearm muscles move the hands and bend the fingers.

Sartorius muscle, the longest in the human body, flexes the knee and hip joint.

Quadriceps at the front of the leg extend the knee joint.

Muscles in the lower leg extend the toes and bend the foot at the ankle.

Muscles inside the foot help you walk and run.

MUSCULAR SYSTEM

More than 600 muscles make up the human body. Many are attached to bones to help you move, but other types of muscle line internal organs and help the heart pump blood around the body.

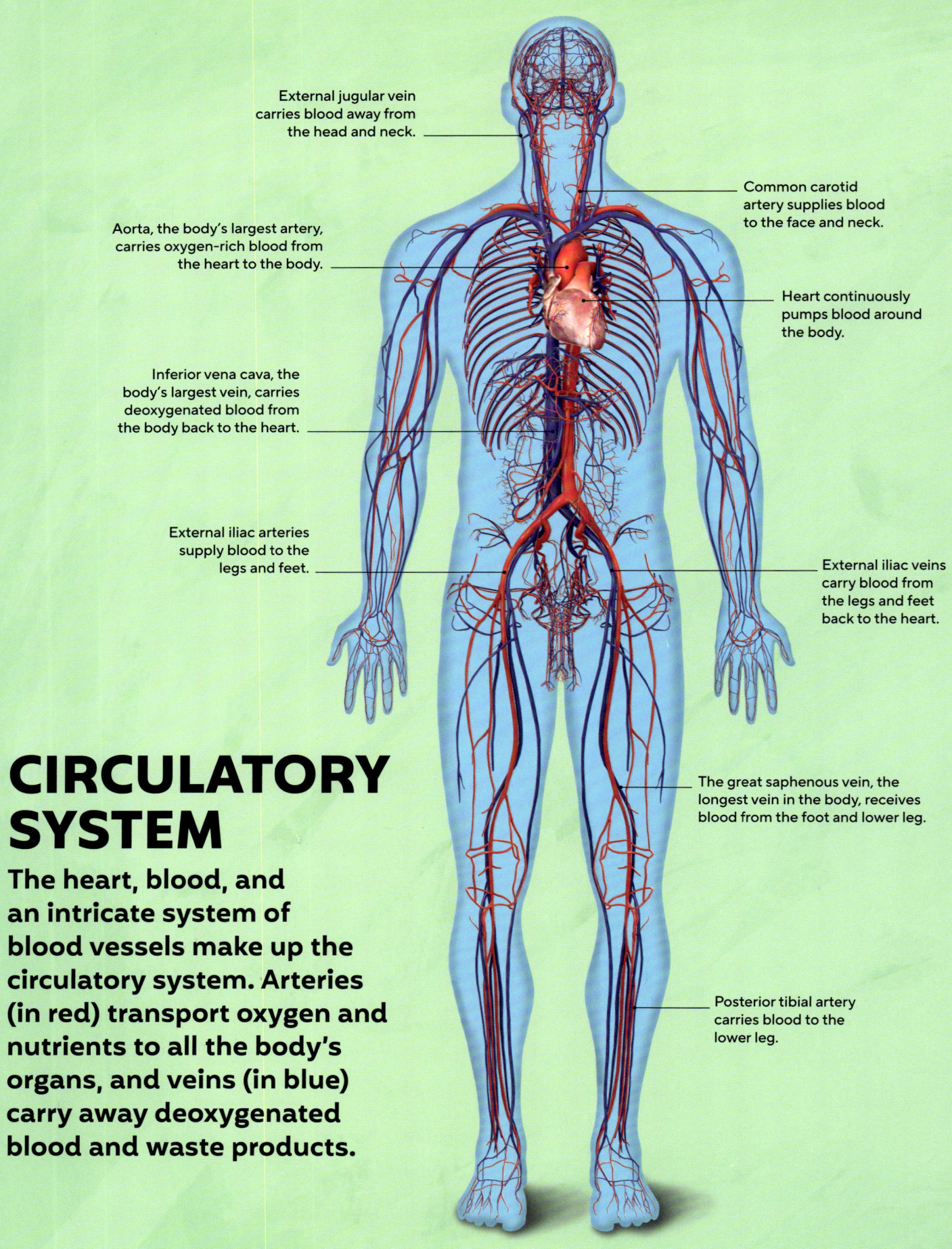

CIRCULATORY SYSTEM

The heart, blood, and an intricate system of blood vessels make up the circulatory system. Arteries (in red) transport oxygen and nutrients to all the body's organs, and veins (in blue) carry away deoxygenated blood and waste products.

External jugular vein carries blood away from the head and neck.

Common carotid artery supplies blood to the face and neck.

Aorta, the body's largest artery, carries oxygen-rich blood from the heart to the body.

Heart continuously pumps blood around the body.

Inferior vena cava, the body's largest vein, carries deoxygenated blood from the body back to the heart.

External iliac arteries supply blood to the legs and feet.

External iliac veins carry blood from the legs and feet back to the heart.

The great saphenous vein, the longest vein in the body, receives blood from the foot and lower leg.

Posterior tibial artery carries blood to the lower leg.

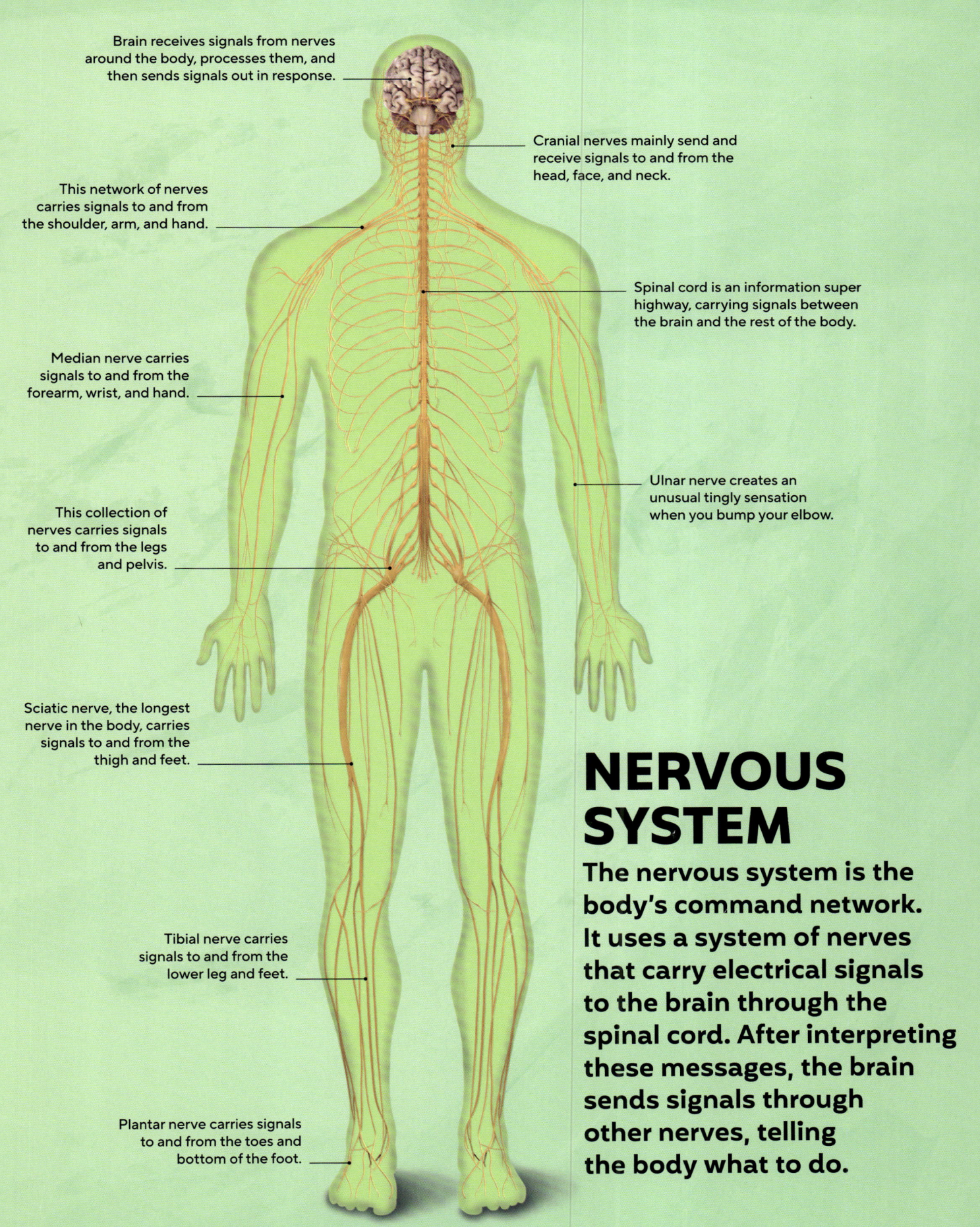

NERVOUS SYSTEM

The nervous system is the body's command network. It uses a system of nerves that carry electrical signals to the brain through the spinal cord. After interpreting these messages, the brain sends signals through other nerves, telling the body what to do.

- Brain receives signals from nerves around the body, processes them, and then sends signals out in response.
- Cranial nerves mainly send and receive signals to and from the head, face, and neck.
- This network of nerves carries signals to and from the shoulder, arm, and hand.
- Spinal cord is an information super highway, carrying signals between the brain and the rest of the body.
- Median nerve carries signals to and from the forearm, wrist, and hand.
- Ulnar nerve creates an unusual tingly sensation when you bump your elbow.
- This collection of nerves carries signals to and from the legs and pelvis.
- Sciatic nerve, the longest nerve in the body, carries signals to and from the thigh and feet.
- Tibial nerve carries signals to and from the lower leg and feet.
- Plantar nerve carries signals to and from the toes and bottom of the foot.

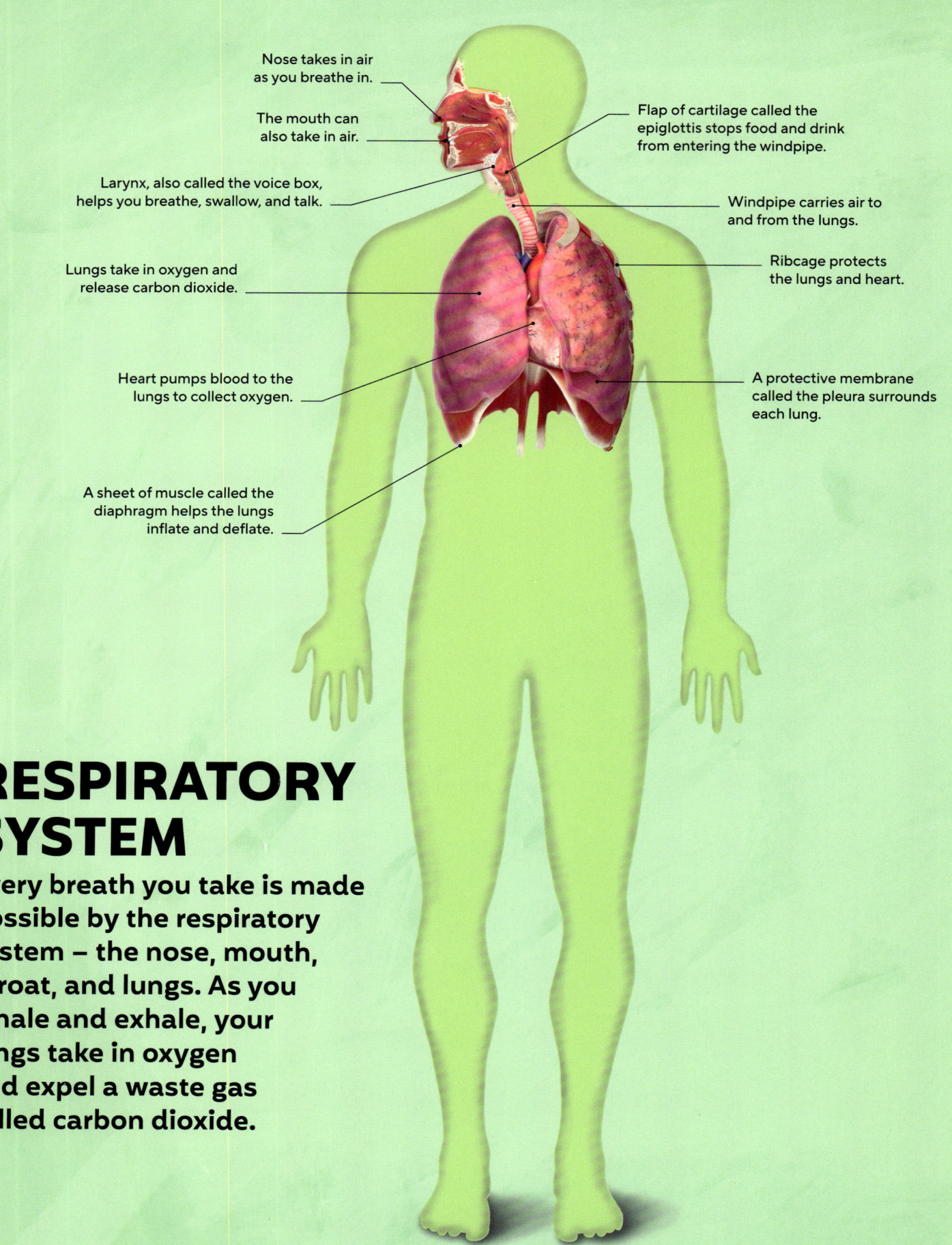

Nose takes in air as you breathe in.

The mouth can also take in air.

Larynx, also called the voice box, helps you breathe, swallow, and talk.

Lungs take in oxygen and release carbon dioxide.

Heart pumps blood to the lungs to collect oxygen.

A sheet of muscle called the diaphragm helps the lungs inflate and deflate.

Flap of cartilage called the epiglottis stops food and drink from entering the windpipe.

Windpipe carries air to and from the lungs.

Ribcage protects the lungs and heart.

A protective membrane called the pleura surrounds each lung.

RESPIRATORY SYSTEM

Every breath you take is made possible by the respiratory system — the nose, mouth, throat, and lungs. As you inhale and exhale, your lungs take in oxygen and expel a waste gas called carbon dioxide.

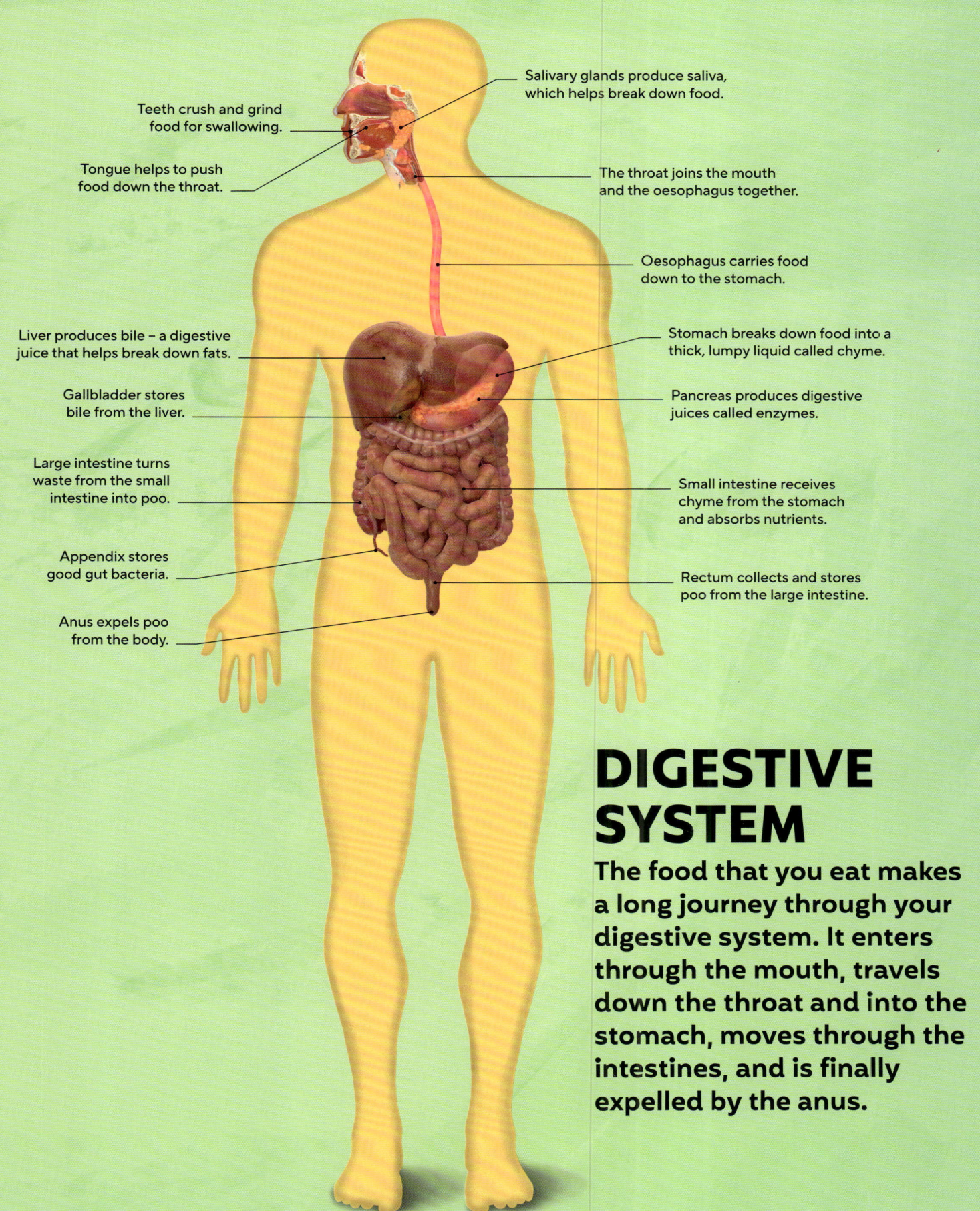

REPRODUCTIVE SYSTEMS

A new life is created by the organs in our reproductive system. Although a male and a female have different reproductive organs, both are needed to make a baby.

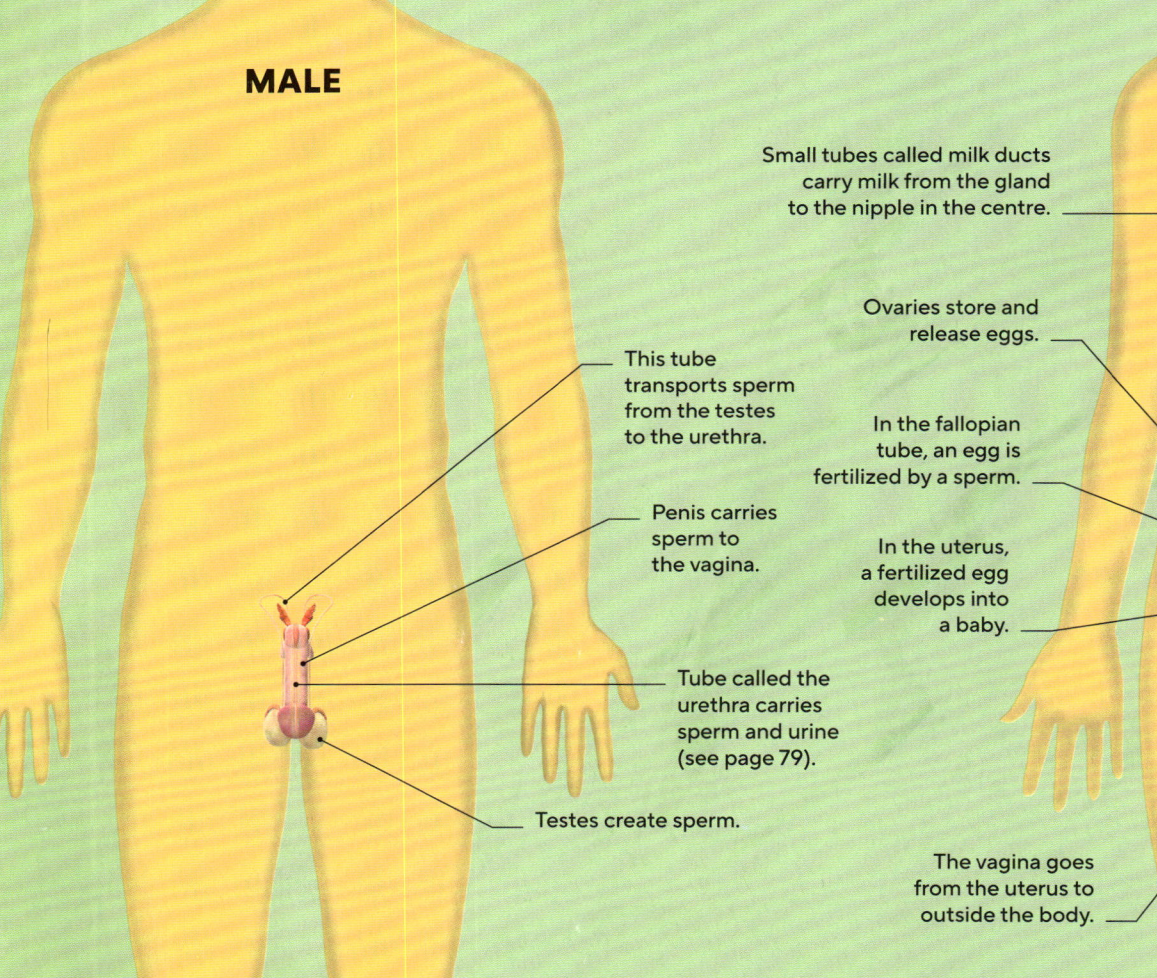

MALE

- This tube transports sperm from the testes to the urethra.
- Penis carries sperm to the vagina.
- Tube called the urethra carries sperm and urine (see page 79).
- Testes create sperm.

FEMALE

- Small tubes called milk ducts carry milk from the gland to the nipple in the centre.
- Ovaries store and release eggs.
- In the fallopian tube, an egg is fertilized by a sperm.
- In the uterus, a fertilized egg develops into a baby.
- The vagina goes from the uterus to outside the body.

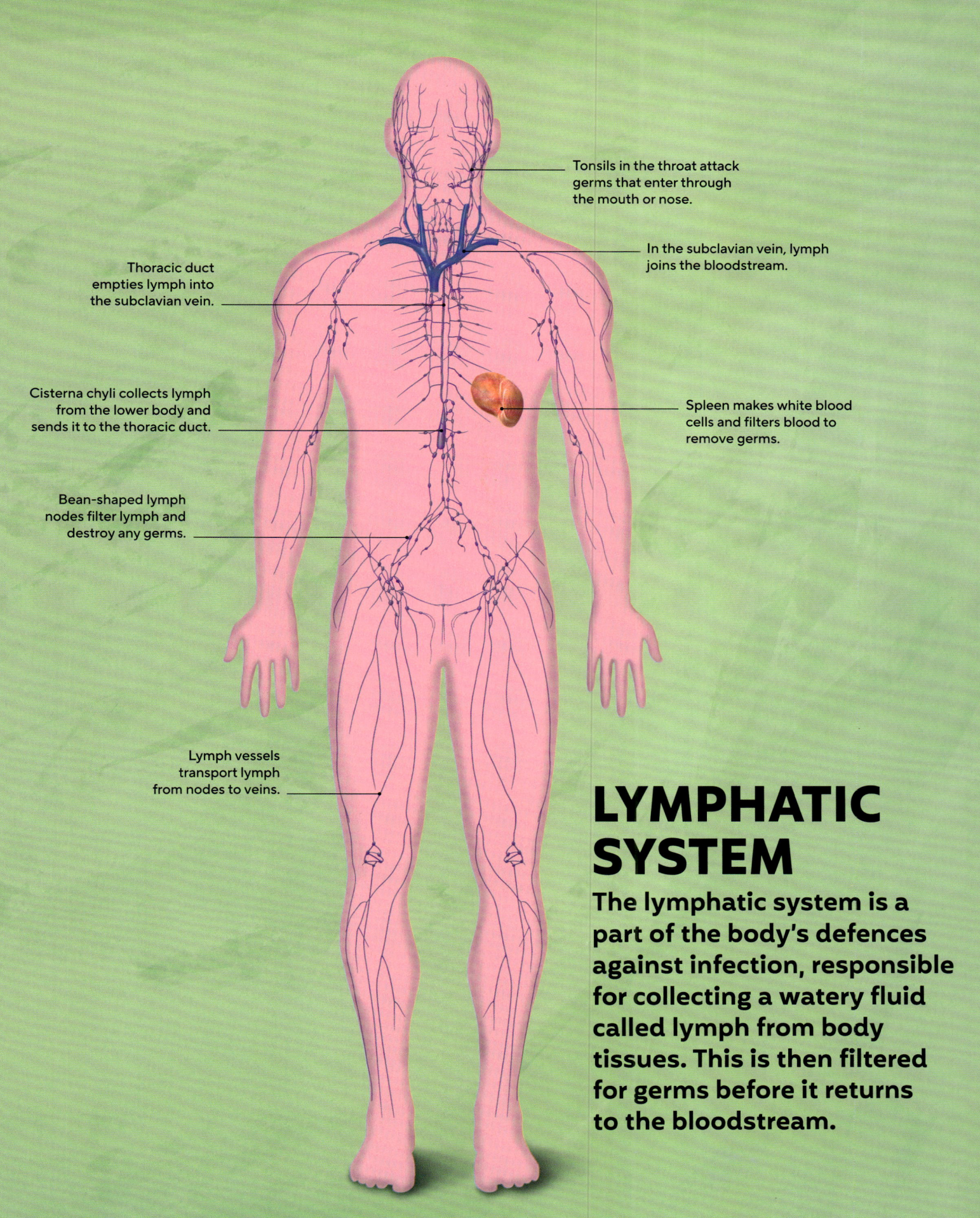

LYMPHATIC SYSTEM

The lymphatic system is a part of the body's defences against infection, responsible for collecting a watery fluid called lymph from body tissues. This is then filtered for germs before it returns to the bloodstream.

- Tonsils in the throat attack germs that enter through the mouth or nose.
- In the subclavian vein, lymph joins the bloodstream.
- Thoracic duct empties lymph into the subclavian vein.
- Cisterna chyli collects lymph from the lower body and sends it to the thoracic duct.
- Spleen makes white blood cells and filters blood to remove germs.
- Bean-shaped lymph nodes filter lymph and destroy any germs.
- Lymph vessels transport lymph from nodes to veins.

LOOKING INSIDE YOUR BODY

From X-rays to ultrasounds, doctors use many different types of scans to peer inside the body. They are used to check that your bones, muscles, organs, and tissues are healthy.

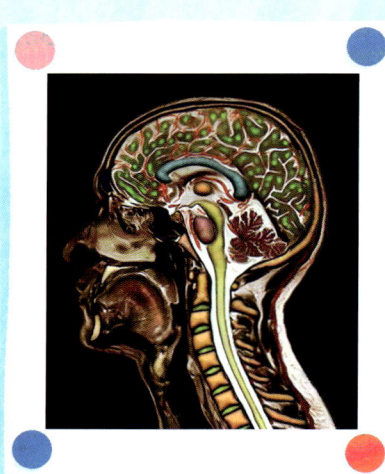

MRI SCAN
To look at soft tissues, such as the heart, liver, and blood vessels, doctors take an MRI (magnetic resonance imaging) scan. This uses strong magnets and radio waves to produce clear images of inside the body. The MRI scan above shows a cross-section image of the brain and spinal cord.

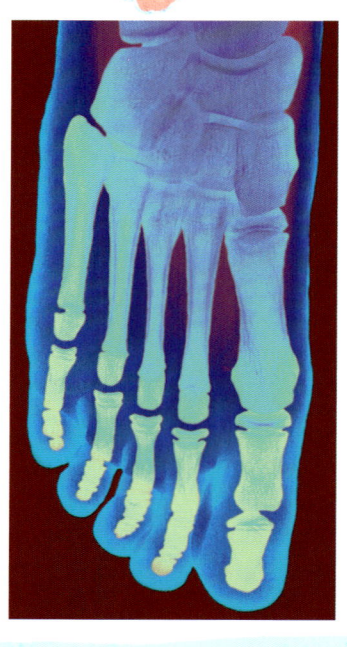

X-RAY IMAGING
Mainly used to examine your bones and joints, X-rays create images using radiation that passes through the body. X-ray radiation cannot pass through dense, solid parts of the body such as bone. This is why these areas appear white, such as the bones of the foot in the image above.

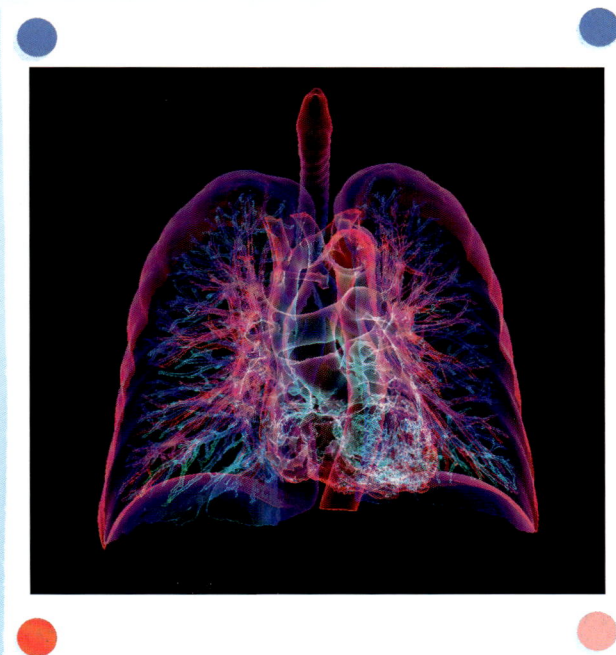

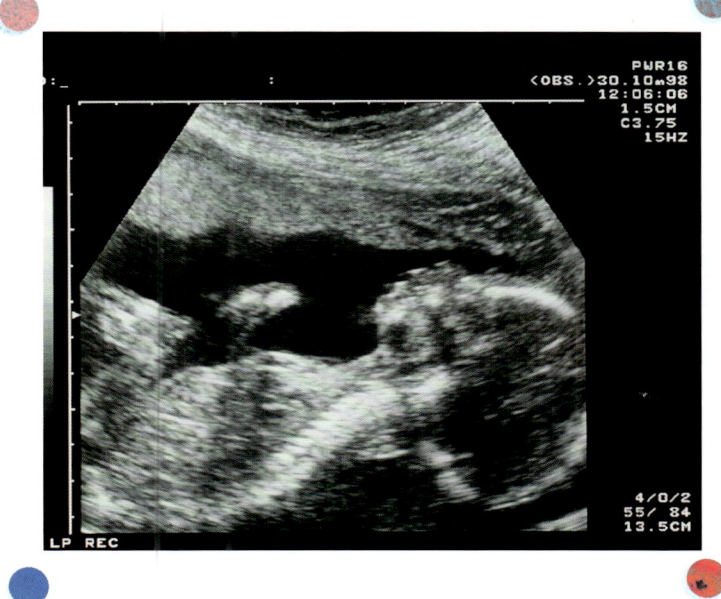

CT SCAN

A combination of an X-ray and computer imaging is called a CT (computed tomography) scan. Used to create 3D images of the inside of your body, including bones, organs, muscles, and soft tissues, CT scans show more detail than a standard X-ray. First an X-ray takes images of the body from different angles, and then a computer digitally combines these images to form a 3D CT scan. The image above shows a CT scan of the heart and lungs.

ULTRASOUND SCAN

An ultrasound scan uses a type of sound wave to produce real-time pictures of soft tissues and organs in your body. Ultrasound scans are often used during pregnancies to check how a baby is developing, but they can also show other organs, such as the heart, eyes, and brain. An ultrasound picture, such as the one above showing a fetus in the womb, is called a sonogram.

YOUR **HEART BEATS** AROUND **100,000 TIMES**.

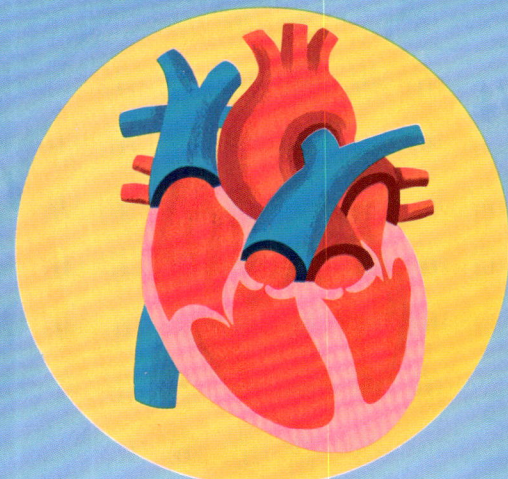

YOUR MOUTH PRODUCES UP TO **1 LITRE (1.75 PINTS)** OF SALIVA.

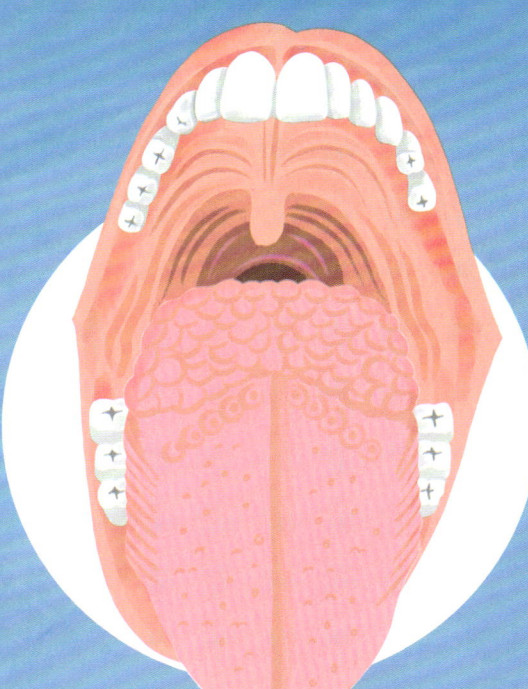

YOUR DAY IN NUMBERS

Over the course of one day, your body does a staggering amount of work – producing bodily fluids, circulating blood and other substances, and growing ever so slightly. All of this adds up over your lifetime!

YOU YAWN BETWEEN 5 AND **20 TIMES**, WITH EACH LASTING **AROUND 5 SECONDS**.

YOUR **FINGERNAILS GROW** JUST **0.1 MM** (0.004 IN).

YOU SPEND AROUND **8 HOURS SLEEPING**, ADDING UP TO **ONE-THIRD** OF YOUR LIFE!

AROUND **5 LITRES (8 PINTS)** OF **BLOOD** ARE CONTINUOUSLY **PUMPED AROUND YOUR BODY.**

YOUR BLADDER PRODUCES AROUND **1.7 LITRES (3 PINTS) OF URINE.**

BLOOD PASSES THROUGH THE **KIDNEYS** AND IS FILTERED **300 TIMES.**

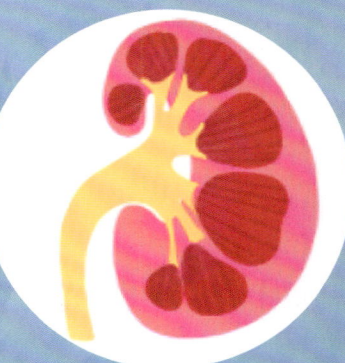

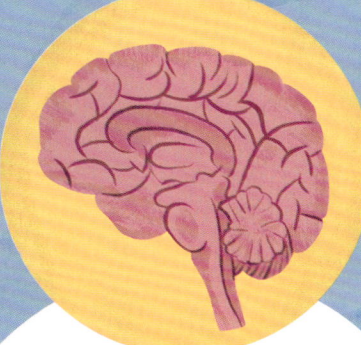

YOUR **BRAIN USES AROUND 20%** OF YOUR BODY'S ENERGY, DESPITE MAKING UP JUST **2% OF YOUR BODY WEIGHT!**

YOU SHED AROUND FIVE BILLION **SKIN CELLS.**

YOUR EYES **BLINK UP TO 43,200 TIMES.**

GLOSSARY

Adrenaline
A hormone that prepares your body for sudden action in times of danger or excitement. Adrenaline is produced by glands on top of the kidneys.

Air pressure
The weight of the atmosphere pressing down on you.

Allergy
An illness caused by an overreaction of the body's immune system to a normally harmless substance.

Amino acid
A simple molecule used by the body to build proteins. Proteins in food are broken down into amino acids by the digestive system.

Anus
The opening at the end of the digestive system, through which waste from digestion (poo) leaves the body.

Artery
A blood vessel that carries blood away from your heart to your body's tissues and organs.

Bacterium (pl. Bacteria)
A small type of microorganism. Bacteria live everywhere. Some types cause disease in humans, but some help to keep your body functioning properly.

Blood
A liquid tissue containing several types of cell. Blood carries oxygen, salts, nutrients, minerals, and hormones around your body. It also collects waste for disposal, such as carbon dioxide that is breathed out by your lungs.

Bloodstream
The flow of blood around your body in the circulatory system.

Blood vessel
Any tube that carries blood around your body.

Bone
A strong, hard body part made chiefly of calcium minerals. There are 206 bones in an adult skeleton.

Braille
A system of touch reading and writing for blind or partially sighted people.

Brain stem
The part of the base of your brain that connects to your spinal cord.

Capillary
The smallest type of blood vessel, which connects veins and arteries together. Your body contains thousands of kilometres of capillaries.

Carbohydrate
A food group that includes sugars and starches that provide your body's main energy supply.

Cartilage
A tough, flexible type of connective tissue that helps support your body and covers the ends of bones in joints.

Central nervous system
Your brain and spinal cord together make up your central nervous system, which is one of the two main parts of the nervous system.

Cerebellum
A small, cauliflower-shaped structure at the base of the back of your brain that helps to coordinate body movements and balance.

Cerebral cortex
The deeply folded, outer layer of your brain. It is used for thinking, memory, movement, language, attention, and processing sensory information.

Chemical
A substance that might occur in nature or be manufactured. Chemicals are all around you and in your body.

Chromosome
One of 46 thread-like packages of DNA found in the nucleus of body cells.

Circadian rhythm
The 24-hour cycles that are part of the body's internal clock.

Computed tomography (CT) scanning
An imaging technique that uses X-rays to produce 2D and 3D images of internal body organs.

136

Cornea
The thin, transparent front part of the eye that covers the iris and pupil.

Deoxyribonucleic acid (DNA)
A long molecule found inside the nucleus of body cells. DNA contains coded instructions that control how your body grows and develops.

Dermis
Middle layer of skin, between the epidermis (top layer) and hypodermis (bottom layer).

Diaphragm
The thin, dome-shaped muscle under your ribcage that helps you breathe and separates the lungs from your stomach and intestines.

Digestion
The process that breaks down food into tiny particles that your body can absorb and use.

Digestive system
Where digestions happens, beginning at the mouth and ending at the anus. Food passes through the oesophagus, stomach, small intestine, and large intestine in the digestive system.

Emotions
Feelings you experience, such as anger, fear, and joy.

Endocrine gland
A gland, such as the pituitary gland, that releases hormones into your blood.

Enzyme
A chemical that speeds up digestion in the digestive system.

Epiglottis
A flap of cartilage that stops food going down your windpipe and into your lungs.

Evaporation
What happens to water or another liquid when it is heated and changes state from a liquid to a gas.

Evolution
The way that living things adapt and change over many generations to become new species.

Fat
A substance found in many foods that provides energy and important ingredients for cells. The layer of cells just under the skin is full of fat.

Fetus
The name given to a baby developing in the uterus from the ninth week after fertilization until it is born.

Fever
A rise in body temperature above the normal range.

Friction
A force between two surfaces that slide against each other.

Fluid
A liquid or a gas, which flows and takes the shape of a container it is in.

Genes
Instructions that control the way your body develops and works. Genes are passed on from parents to their children and are part of your DNA in the centre of your body cells.

Genetics
The study of how genes and associated traits are passed down from one generation to the next.

Germ
A tiny, living thing that can get into your body and make you ill. Bacteria and viruses are types of germ.

Gland
A group of specialized cells that make and release a particular substance, such as a hormone.

Gravity
The force that pulls objects towards the ground.

Hormone
A chemical produced by glands in order to change the way a different part of the body works. Hormones are carried by the blood.

Hypothalamus
A small structure in the base of your brain that controls many body activities, including temperature and thirst.

Immune system
A collection of cells and tissues that protect the body from disease by searching out and destroying germs and cancer cells.

Infection
If germs invade your body and begin to multiply, they cause an infection. Some diseases are caused by infections. Your immune system is designed to fight off infections.

Inheritance
The passing down of genes and characteristics, such as eye colour, from parent to child.

137

Irritant
A substance that causes pain, itching, or discomfort, such as smoke in the eyes.

Joint
A connection between two bones.

Ligament
A tough band of tissue that connects bones where they meet at the joints.

Lymphatic system
A network of vessels that collect fluid from body tissues and filter it for germs.

Magnetic resonance imaging (MRI)
A scanning technique that uses magnetism, radio waves, and a computer to produce images of the body's insides.

Melanin
A brown-black pigment that is found in your skin, hair, and eyes and gives them their colour.

Melanocyte
A cell that produces melanin.

Mind
The thoughts, feelings, beliefs, ideas, and sense of self generated by the brain.

Mitochondrion (pl. Mitochondria)
Tiny structures found inside cells that release energy from sugar.

Mucus
Slippery liquid found on the inside of your nose, throat, and intestines.

Muscle
A body part that contracts (gets shorter) to move your bones or internal organs. Muscles are made of lots of fibres.

Muscle fibre
A muscle cell.

Nerve cell
See neuron.

Nerve impulse
A tiny electrical signal that is transmitted along a nerve cell at high speed.

Neurodivergent
Individuals whose brain works and processes information differently from what is considered typical.

Neuron
Another word for nerve cell. Neurons carry information around your body as electrical signals.

Neurotransmitter
A chemical created by nerve cells (neurons) that relays signals across the tiny gaps (synapses) between one neuron and another.

Nucleus
The control centre of a cell, which contains its DNA.

Nutrients
The basic chemicals that make up food. Your body uses nutrients for fuel, growth, and repair.

Oesophagus
A tube forming the part of the digestive system that connects the mouth and the stomach.

Organ
A group of tissues that form a body part designed for a specific job. Your heart is an organ and so is your skin.

Organelle
A structure in a cell that carries out an essential role.

Oxygen
A gas, found in air, that is vital for life. Oxygen is breathed in, absorbed by the blood, and used by cells to release energy from glucose (a simple sugar).

Pathogen
A microorganism that causes disease. Pathogens are also called germs and include bacteria and viruses.

Peristalsis
The wave of muscular contractions in the wall of a hollow organ that, for example, pushes food down the oesophagus during swallowing.

Pigment
A material found in cells that gives colour to skin, hair, and eyes.

Proteins
Vital nutrients that help your body build new cells. Food such as meat, fish, and cheese are rich in proteins.

Puberty
The stage of life when children grow into young adults through a series of physical and emotional changes.

Pupil
The black circle in the centre of the eye that lets light in. It is an opening in the iris, the coloured circle around it.

Radiation
Energy that moves from place to place in the form of waves or particles. Light, sound, and heat are all types of radiation.

Radio waves
A form of electromagnetic radiation used in scans and communcation.

Red blood cell
A disc-shaped cell that contains haemoglobin (a protein that carries oxygen and makes your blood red).

Reflex
A rapid, automatic reaction that is out of your control, such as blinking when something moves towards your eyes.

Retina
A layer of light-sensitive neurons lining the back of each eye. The retina captures images and relays them to the brain as electrical signals.

Saliva
The liquid in your mouth. Saliva helps you taste, swallow, and digest food and is produced by glands.

Scanning
Any technique used to create images of soft tissues and organs inside the body.

Sebum
An oily liquid that keeps your hair and skin soft, flexible, and waterproof.

Sensory receptor
A specialized nerve cell that detects a stimulus, such as light, scent, touch, or sound. These cells can also be sensitive to warmth, cold, and pain.

Spinal cord
A column of nerve cells (neurons) that runs down your backbone and connects your brain to the rest of the body.

Surface area
The total surface over which substances and heat can be exchanged.

Sweat
A watery liquid produced by glands in the skin. As it evaporates, sweat cools down the body.

System
A group of organs that work together to perform a set of related functions. Your mouth, stomach, and intestines make up your digestive system.

Tendon
A cord of tough, connective tissue that links muscle to bone.

Time zone
It takes 24 hours for Earth to rotate once on its axis. Using imaginary lines that run from the North to the South Pole, the globe is split into 24 time zones, one for each hour of the day.

Tissue
A group of cells that look and act the same. Muscle is a type of tissue.

Torso
The body apart from the head, neck, arms, and legs.

Ultrasound
An imaging technique that uses inaudible, high-frequency sound waves to produce pictures of a developing baby in the womb or of body tissues.

Uterus
The organ in a woman's body where a baby grows during pregnancy.

Vein
A blood vessel that carries blood towards your heart.

Virus
A kind of germ that invades cells and multiplies inside them. Diseases caused by viruses include the common cold, measles, and influenza.

Vitamins
One of a number of substances, including vitamins A and C, needed in small amounts in your diet to keep your body healthy.

Vocal cords
The small folds of tissue in your voice box that vibrate to create the sounds of speech.

Voice box (Larynx)
A structure at the top of the windpipe that generates sound as you speak. The sound is created by folds of tissue that vibrate as you breathe out.

Water vapour
Water in its gas state.

Waves
A wave transfers energy from one place to another. Waves include light, sound, radiation, and ocean waves.

White blood cell
Any of the colourless blood cells that play a role in your immune system.

Windpipe (Trachea)
The main airway leading from the back of your throat to your lungs.

X-rays
A form of radiation that reveals bones when projected through the body onto photographic film.

INDEX

Page numbers in **bold** show the pages with the main information.

A

acid 106
acne 116
adrenal glands 88
adrenaline 88
air pressure 96
allergies 52, **86–87**
altitude **24–25**, 96
alveoli 22, 89
amygdala 45, 88, 118
anger 13
antihistamines 52, 53
antiperspirant 15
antiseptic wipes 52, 60
anus 47, 93, 129
anxiety **44–45**
aorta 119, 126
armpits 15, 51
arms 43, 73
arrector pili 31
arteries 72, 97, 119, 126

B

bacteria 14, 19, 108–109, 117
bad breath 19
ball and socket joints 73
bandages 53
belly button 60
biceps 10, 49, 125
bile 107
birthmarks 117
bladder 79, 135
blinking 11, 57, 135
blisters 26
blood 49, 95
    cells 17, 51, 61, 131
    pressure 43, 113
blood vessels
    arteries 72, 97, 119, 126
    capillaries 22, 89, 97
    veins 43, 97, 119, 126
body systems **124–131**
bones 28–29, 48, 58–59, 124
    broken 63
    'funny' bone 26
    growth 121
braces 20
braille 81
brain **56–57**, 81, 110, 135
    hemispheres 67, 101
    hypothalamus 30, 37
breathing **22–23**, 34, 73, 74
bruises 62
bum 80
burns 63, 95
burps 107

C

capillaries 22, 89, 97
capsaicin 64
cardiac muscle 16, 118
cartilage 23, 84, 121
cells **16–17**, 109, 120
    brain 110
    blood 17, 51, 61, 131
cerebellum 67
chewing 65, 104
chyme 46, 106, 107
circadian rhythm 12, 111
circulatory system 16, **126**
cochlea 66
colds 51
cold weather **30–31**
collagen 92
communication **82–83**, 115
competitiveness 68
cones 42
constipation 47
cornea 111
corpus callosum 67
cortex 56, 110
cramp 63
crying 91, 100
CT scans 133
cuticles 10
cytoplasm 16, 109

D

default mode network 81
dehydration 79, 95
dentine 94
dermis 15, 61, 95
diaphragm 34, 37, 128
diarrhea 47
    digestive system 39, 46–47, **106–107, 129**
dizziness 24, **38–39**
DNA 17, **70–71**, 120
dominant hands 101
double helix 71
dreams 118
drinking **36–37**, 79, 106
dust allergies 86
dyslexia 57

E

ears 38, 96
    ear canal 57, 96
    eardrum 66, 96
eating 28, **64–65, 104–105**
E. coli bacteria 108–109

elastin 92
electrical signals 35, 56
emotions
    anxiety **44–45**
    envy **68–69**
    fear 88–89
    grumpiness 12–13
    happiness **102–103**
    sadness **90–91**
    tiredness 12–13
enamel 94
endoplasmic reticulum 17
endorphins 102, 112
envy 68–69
enzymes 107
epidermis 15, 40, 63, 95
epiglottis 65, 128
Eustachian tube 96
evaporation 35, 94
excitement 112
exercise 26–27
    gymnastics 48–49
    running 34–35
    swimming 72–73
eyebrows 115
eyes 39, 42, 56, 111
    blinking 11, 57
    eyelids 57
    pupils 88–89, 111

F

facial expressions 83
farts 93
fear **88–89**
feelings *see* emotions
feet 14, 59, 60
female body 47, 78, **130**
femur 27, 58
fibres 35, 48, 92
fibrin 61
fidgeting 59
'fight or flight mode' 44, 88–89

fingers 14, 42, 67, 81
    fingernails 114, 134
    fingerprints 101
first aid kit **52–53**
flagellum 108
flavour 97, 105
floating 73
fluoride 18
foetuses 133
follicles 114, 115, 116
food allergies 87
fractures 63
freckles 116
frostbite 25
'funny' bone 26

G

gaming **110–111**
gas exchange 22
genes 65, 92
    see also DNA
germs 51, 61, 85
G-force **112–113**
glands 15, 51, 100
goosebumps 31
gravity 40–41, 60
growth 115, **120–121**
grumpiness **12–13**
gums 20, 21

H

hair 10, 92, 114
    goosebumps 31
hands 30, 42, 89, 101
happiness **102–103**
headaches 28
head size 120
hearing 57, 66
heart 16, 50, 134
    heartbeat 34, 44, 89
height 23, 121
hiccups 37

high altitudes 24–25, 96
high speed **112–113**
hormones 74, 83, 120
hot weather **94–95**
humerus 27, 73, 124
hunger 64
hydration 79, 95
hypermobility 48
hypothalamus 30, 37
hypothermia 24

I

ice packs 52
illness 24, **50–53**, 85
immune system 19, 86
infections 51, 52, 131
injuries 52–53, **60–63**
inner ear 38, 66
insect stings 53, 86
intestines 39, 46, 108–109
    large 129
    small 64, 107, 129

J

jaw 11, 65, 104, 124
jealousy 69
jet lag 96
joints 42, 48, 58, 73

K

kidneys 78, 95, 135
knees 58, 61
knuckles 58

L

lacrimal glands 11
language 81, 83
larynx 82, 128
laughing 102
lens 111
ligaments 48
limbic system 88
liver 36, 107, 129
lungs 22, 50, 129
lymphatic system 51, **131**

M

male body 79, 83, **130**
mandible 65, 124
mastication 104
medulla 23
meibum 11
melanin 85, 116
melanocyte 85, 92, 95, 116
memories 49, 84, 118
metabolism 46
microbes **108–109**
middle ear 66, 96
milk teeth 18
mitochondria 17
moles 116
motion sickness 39
mouth 37, 64, 134

MRI scans 132
mucus 11, 51, 85
muscle memory 49
muscles
    cardiac 16, 118
    facial 83, 104
    pelvic floor 47
    skeletal 31, 35, 43
muscular system 48, 49, 72, **125**

N

nails 114, 134
nausea **38–39**
neck 23, 51
nephrons 78, 95
nerves
    auditory 38
    facial 28, 104, 105
    olfactory 84, 97
    optic 39, 56
    spinal 23, 100
    ulnar 26
nervous system 14, 23, 61, **127**
neurodivergence 57
neurons 101
nodes 51, 131
nose 51, 64, 84–85
    nosebleeds 29
nucleus, cell 17, 120

O

oesophagus 104, 107, 129
olfactory bulb 84, 97
onions 100

organelles 16
otolith organs 38
oxygen 49, 119

P

painkillers 53
pain receptors 28
pancreas 107, 129
pandiculation 11
papillae 105
peanut allergies 87
pelvis 27, 59
    female 47, 78
    male 79
peristalsis 64, 104
pigment 85, 92, 116–117
pili 109
pimples 115
pins and needles 59
pituitary gland 120
plaque 18, 21
plasma 61
platelets 61
pollen allergies 86
pons 23
poo 46–47
pores 15, 35, 94, 115
proteins 17, 117
puberty 83, 116, 121
pulp 94
pupils 88–89, 111

R

rectum 47, 129
red blood cells 17, 51, 61
reflexes 85, 100, 111
reproductive systems **130**
respiratory system **128**
retainers 20
retina 39, 111, 112
ribcage 22, 27, 124
rods 42
rumbles, stomach 64, 107

142

S

sacrum 59
sadness **90–91**
saliva 37, 104, 129
scans, body **132–133**
sebum 115
senses **84–85**
serum 26
shivering 31
shoulders 73
sickness 24, **50–53**, 85
sign language 83
sinuses 113
skeletal system 26–27, 58–59, **124**
    see also bones
skin 15, 30, **116–117**
    melanin 85
    pores 15, 35, 94, 115
    sunburn 95
    wrinkles 14, 92
sleep 10, **118–119**, 120, 134
    patterns 41, 111
    tiredness 12–13
smell, sense of 84, 97, 105
sneezing 85
snoring 119
snot 85
snow blindness 25
soap 15
social mirroring 11
space travel **40–41**
sphincters 47
spicy foods 41, 64, 65
spinal cord 23, 100
spindles 11
spine 23, 27, 41, 124
spit (saliva) 37, 104, 129
spleen 51, 131
splinters 62
spots 115
static shocks 27
stethoscope 50
stitch (side pain) 35
stomach 104, 106–107, 129
    rumbling 64, 107
stretching 10–11, 48
sunburn 53, 95
sunscreen 53
swallowing 65, 96, 104
sweat 15, 35, 89, 94
swimming **72–73**

T

tailbone 80
taste buds 41, 97, 105
tear ducts 11
teeth **18–22**, 31, 93, 94
temperature, body 30, 50, 94
tendons 10, 42, 67
thermometers 53
thumbs 42
thyroid 46
tibia 27, 58, 124
tiredness **12–13**
toilet **46–47**, **78–79**
tongue 19, 105, 129
tonsils 19
toothache 21
touch 100, 101
triceps 49
tunnel vision 112

U

ulnar nerve 26, 127
ultrasound scans 133
underwater 73, **74–75**
urethra 78–79
urination 74, **78–79**, 95, 135
uterus 130
UV (ultraviolet) rays 53, 95
uvula 19

V

valves 43, 119
vapour rub 53
veins 43, 97, 119, 126
verrucas 117
vertebrae 23
vesicles 17
virtual reality 38
viruses 51, 85, 117
vocal cords 37, 82, 83
voicebox 82, 83
vomiting 39

W

waking up **10–11**, 12, 119
warts 117
washing **14–15**, 41
water vapour 35
wee (urination) 74, **78–79**, 95, 135
whispering 82
white blood cells 51, 61, 131
windpipe 65, 82, 128
wisdom teeth 20
wounds 52–53, **60–63**
wrinkled skin 14, 92

X

x-ray scans 132

Y

yawning 11, 96, 134

ACKNOWLEDGEMENTS

The publisher would like to thank the following people for their assistance in the preparation of the book: Zara Kadir for consulting on the emotions spreads; Rona Skene, Michelle Crane, Sam Kennedy, and Georgina Palffy for editorial assistance; Hazel Beynon for proofreading; and Elizabeth Wise for the index.

The publisher would like to thank the following for their kind permission to reproduce their photographs:

132 Science Photo Library: Du Cane Medical Imaging Ltd (cr); Medical Media Images (cl). 133 Science Photo Library: (tr); K H Fung (cla)

(Key: a-above; b-below/bottom; c-centre; f-far; l-left; r-right; t-top)